100 INSTANT TALKS

100 INSTANT TALKS FOR ALL OCCASIONS

Ian Knox

David C Cook

Kingsway Communications Ltd
Lottbridge Drove, Eastbourne BN23 6NT, UK

David C. Cook
4050 Lee Vance View, Colorado Springs, CO 80918, USA

David C. Cook Distribution Canada
55 Woodslee Avenue, Paris, Ontario, Canada N3L 3E5

David C. Cook and the graphic circle C logo
are registered trademarks of Cook Communications Ministries.

Bible quotations are from the following versions:
Unidentified = New International Version, © 1973, 1978, 1984
by the International Bible Society.
TLB = The Living Bible, © 1971 Tyndale House Publishers
RSV = Revised Standard Version, © 1946, 1952 by the Division of Christian
Education of the National Council of the Churches of Christ in the USA
GNB = Good News Bible, © American Bible Society 1976, 1994
KJV = King James (Authorized) Version, crown copyright
NEB = New English Bible, © Delegates of the Oxford University Press and
the Syndics of the Cambridge University Press 1961, 1970
Moffatt = A New Translation of the Bible by James Moffatt 1913, 1924,
1926, 1935, published by Hodder & Stoughton
Jerusalem = Jerusalem Bible, © 1966, 1967, 1968 by Darton, Longman &
Todd Ltd and Doubleday & Co Inc
Amplified = Amplified Bible, © 1954, 1958, 1962, 1964, 1965, 1987
by The Lockman Foundation

ISBN 978 1 842913 49 9

Front cover design by CCD; photo: Corbis

Printed in the USA
First Edition 2008

1 2 3 4 5 6 7 8 9 10

Contents

Start Here

Welcome to the wonderful world of preaching! If these opening words bring a reaction of 'if only', here are some which should cause a degree of relief: Don't panic. This book aims to be a rescue act for Christian preachers and speakers, even – and perhaps especially – in a last-minute crisis.

If you have a reasonable time to prepare a talk and wonder where to start, then the substantial introductory chapter to my book *100 Instant Faith-Sharing Talks* will give some guidelines on the general theme of putting a talk together. It was the considerable success of that book which encouraged the publishers to commission this tome.

The concept is simple. The church leader calls you on a Friday night. 'The preacher's dropped out for Sunday: I need you to do it. The theme is. . .' It is very possible that you yourself are the leader and, for whatever reason, it is now Friday and Sunday's sermon is not started. It may not be the Sunday sermon. It could be the men's breakfast, the ladies' lunch, the senior citizens' 'Songs of Praise' or the junior school assembly. There is one common factor: you are the speaker and you need a talk right now. So – here it is! Whatever the panic, this book hopes to rescue you.

As you look at these 100 talks you will find a similar style in the layout for each one. This has been done quite deliberately, to make understanding and absorbing them as easy as possible. Compared with *100 Instant Faith-Sharing Talks*, a great deal more detail is given, again with the understanding that last-minute help may be being sought.

At the beginning of each talk is the heading 'WHEN:'. The answer then given is by no means exclusive. A quick glance at the very first talk will show that it could be used on many occasions, not just on January 1. Most talks can be adapted to a multitude of situations. With 100 talks in this book, a very desperate – or lazy – preacher may have two years' worth of help here! The indexes have further suggestions as to when talks can be used.

The dates and seasons are also only a guide, particularly if liturgical seasons are not followed in your church. These talks (up to number 38) can be given at other times. Look at talk 34, 'Sunday Before Advent'. It is a great day to celebrate the liturgical 'Feast of Christ the King' but he can be presented on any day!

How to get going

The first task is to decide what is the occasion for the talk and who is likely to form the audience/congregation. These two factors will determine which talk is then chosen. Are you looking for a talk to fit a particular Sunday or other special day (e.g. Palm Sunday), or are you wanting a theme ('Giving'), or is it a special event (a wedding)? Will those present be primarily Christians or will a considerable percentage of your hearers still be on their way to a real faith? If the latter make up your congregation on a regular basis, do get a copy of that other 100 book. However, there is a section in this book which covers such an eventuality (talks 94 to 100) because nothing is more vital than helping others to become true Christians.

Next, read through the talk you have chosen, especially going through the suggested Bible passage. If you are not speaking in a church service, will it be appropriate to read this at the event, or would it be better to bring it into the context of what you say without specifically reading it verse for verse? As you look at the talk and Bible reading, make some notes for yourself. It would be a bit of a giveaway to have this book in the pulpit. . . Work out where you are heading, leave out the bits which do not work for you, add your own ideas, quotations and illustrations and *voilà*! You have a talk.

You will need to consider how long your talk should be. This will depend on a variety of factors, not least how well you can 'hold' your audience and how much they can tackle. The art is to finish two minutes before they turn off! Concentration spans are not great, so try not to go on too long. The shorter you plan to be, the more you will need to stick to the outline. For a very short talk, pick one salient point and make it well. Most talks in this book could be given well in 20 minutes, but there is flexibility for honing down to ten or expanding to whatever is appropriate.

A number of talks lend themselves to being part of a mini-series, so you can have a month or so of sermons which fit together. There are two sets which have been deliberately written to do this, even though they have been separated in the book to fit into a liturgical or thematic context.

The first comes under the heading, 'What is the Gospel?' Talks 27, 20, 31 and 38 – in that order – follow the good news through Matthew, Mark, Luke and John. They can be given individually at the appropriate season. However, collectively their themes run like this:

- Matthew: God with us, and always with us.
- Mark: develops this theme, showing that because God is with us, heaven is with us and we can go to heaven.
- Luke: with heaven come its great features of power and peace. We can have a new way to live.
- John: look at the previous three and then, believe it, by trusting the Jesus who is 'God with us' (full circle to Matthew).

The second mini-series is a walk through Psalm 103. These are talks 62, 42, 59 and 48, again in that order. This psalm tackles four key themes in life, namely healing, forgiveness, bereavement and praise. It would work well at those times of the year when the liturgy is somewhat quieter, such as during the long stretch from Trinity Sunday to Harvest, or leading up to Advent.

You will discover that other talks lend themselves to forming their own mini-series because of their length. Talk 33, on Psalm 107, would make a five- or six-week series with Remembrance Sunday in the middle. Talks 1, 22, 45 and 56 would also divide into several talks. Talks 42 and 43 could be given on consecutive weeks, as could talks 44 and 45. There is no reason why other talks could not be divided or united.

Quotations

With several hundred quotes in this book, a word of explanation may be appreciated. First, the vast majority are from the Bible, as the Bible Index at the back of this book will show. There is no greater source for our speaking and preaching. When we grow weary of the Bible, we need a sabbatical. Use God's word frequently, accepting God's promise in Isaiah 55:11, 'My word . . . will not return to me empty.'

As for the many other quotations (some 550 in all, from over 400 sources), every speaker realises that other people say things better, more pithily and in a more apposite and appropriate way. To speak personally, I have been keeping my own Quotes Book since 1968, which I have decided to give away piecemeal in this new book. Even then, some quotes would not fit. These include my very favourite, from a recent pope. He was asked, 'How many people work at the Vatican?' He replied, 'About half.' Classic. Another beauty comes from a different churchmanship. The former Director of the Moody Bible Institute, Dr George Sweeting, said at the 1986 Congress of Evangelism in Amsterdam, 'We need to make hell gasp for breath.'

If your reaction is that this is stealing, the only defence is that everyone does it. Look at the New Testament using the Old Testament. Many people quote Billy Graham's delightful reply to the question, 'Why do you say you need to be continually filled with the Holy Spirit?' 'Because I leak!' He got it from an evangelist of many years earlier, D. L. Moody. Who knows where he found it.

We all have our favourites, so no apologies are offered for several quotations from the same author. An example would be the brilliant Bible study books by Professor David Gooding from Northern Ireland. However, you are unlikely to recognise many of the sources, as they are from friends, preachers I have heard and people who, on a particular occasion, had *le mot juste*. Whoever the originator, they had a great way of saying exactly what I would have wanted to say. Use the quotations as you wish – or not. If you want 'the usual suspects', get a couple of good quotations books, one Christian and one secular.

Been there, done that

The inimitable Flanders and Swann, raconteurs and humorists of some years ago, used to jest about car manufacturers wanting cars to be tested after one, two and three years. The joke was that there were even plans being mooted to test the cars before they left the factory. . . I want to give this word of assurance: every one of these talks has already been tested on live audiences, with not one rotten tomato being thrown as a result. They come from a wealth of nearly 50 years of preaching, speaking and personal experience. Especially for those talks on particularly tricky subjects, great care has been given both in preparation and subsequent presentation. To give one example, talk 47 – which looks at other faiths – comes from visits to several places in the world where other faiths predominate, and from working alongside local Christians there.

A final word

This book is written with huge thanks to the very many people whose talks and quotes have contributed. I am extremely grateful to Richard Herkes at Kingsway for his unstinting encouragement. Without the help of my secretary, Lisa Howard; Director of the 40:3 Trust, Darren Burgess; and the wisdom, love and enthusiasm of my wife,

Ruth, this book would not be in your hands now. Ultimately, as Johann Sebastian Bach frequently ended his compositions, 'S.D.G.' – *Soli Deo Gloria* – 'For the glory of God alone'. This book is for God's glory, as all our preaching should be.

And to you, the reader: 'Preach the Word' (2 Timothy 4:2) in the power of the Holy Spirit.

THROUGH THE YEAR

1. January 1: Naming of Jesus

WHEN: January 1: Naming of Jesus. Nine lessons and carols.

WHO: Seekers.

AIM: To show how vital Jesus is, why he came and who he is.

HINT: This talk could be quite long: it could even be used to make its own mini-series of four talks (even more for your money!). In a 'Nine lessons and carols' you may want only to give the main headings and one thought after each. Although the theology is profound, it can be used almost anywhere to explain who Jesus is.

BIBLE READING: John 1:1–18. A second reading could be Isaiah 57:14–19. All verses without references below are from John 1.

OUTLINE: Why do we bother with Jesus? Why is he so important? Four reasons:

1. **Before Jesus: nothing.** Verses 1 and 2 are about Jesus, as verses 14 and 17 show. How can Jesus be 'God' and yet 'with God'?

Quote: 'Happy is he who can receive it as a little child, without attempting to explain it.' (J. C. Ryle)

Refer to Isaiah 57:15 (first part) and Isaiah 55:9. Just because we can't grasp it doesn't make it false: it makes Jesus unique.

Mention a few very famous people known to your hearers (the occasion will decide whom you choose). They each had a beginning. But Jesus was 'in the beginning'.

2. **Without Jesus: nothing.** Verses 3 and 4. Enthuse about the wonders of creation, the greatness of the universe, mountains and oceans, the intricate detail of a butterfly and a snowflake. Never confuse the 'how' with the 'who'.

   Quote/Story: The scientist John Haldane suggested to Monsignor Ronald Knox that in a universe of millions of planets, it was inevitable that life should appear by chance on one of them. Knox replied, 'If Scotland Yard found a body in your cabin trunk, would you tell them, "There are millions of trunks in the world – surely one of them must contain a body"? I think they would still want to know who put it there.'

   Jesus is the Creator. Now come the two great words in verse 11: 'He came', expanded in verse 14a. Which leads to. . .

3. **After Jesus: everything.** Verse 14: Jesus brings:
   (a) Grace. 'Full of grace.' The tragedy is in verses 10 and 11, but Jesus brought his undeserved love.

   Quotes: 'Grace: the reaching out to us of an enabling

love in which we are loved before we are even capable of loving – a love which loves us as we are and for what we may become.' (*The Times*, editorial, Ash Wednesday, 25.2.98)

'Amid the darkness, the light shone, but the darkness did not master it.' (Verse 5, Moffatt)

It took Jesus all the way to the cross.
(b) Truth. 'Full of grace and truth.' The law (verse 17) condemns us: Jesus is the defence lawyer (see also 1 John 2:1).
(c) Glory. 'We have seen his glory': the glory of God. Because of Jesus, we can know God (verse 18). And 2 Corinthians 4:6 is excellent here.

Before Jesus – nothing; after Jesus – everything. Without Jesus – nothing, but:

4. **Within Jesus: everything.** The talk climaxes at verses 12 and 13. The second half of Isaiah 57:15 can be used.

Quote: 'He came into our time that we might go into his eternity.' (Harry Alcker)

Here is our new beginning: the God of creation comes to re-create us, to reconcile us, to make us his children.

Quote: 'These became what they were, not because "they were born like that", not because "it's human nature to live like that", not because men "chose to live like that", but because God himself gave them their new life.' (Alan Dale's paraphrase of verse 13)

Ending: Whether you've made this one talk or four, encourage your hearers to enjoy this amazing relationship with God which Jesus has brought.

2. January 6: Epiphany

WHEN: Epiphany. Nearest Sunday to Epiphany. Christmas. If the references to the gifts are omitted, then any time to almost any audience.

WHO: Seekers.

AIM: To show who Jesus is. This talk takes the three gifts of the Magi as a way of explaining who it was they came to visit and whom we may meet as we come to worship.

BIBLE READING: Matthew 2:1–12. Or (if not using 'gifts' and not Epiphany) John 1:1–14.

OUTLINE:
Opening question: Who is Jesus? Who is this figure who divides history and strides through the years, whose birth we celebrate like no other?

> **Quote:** 'The ancient world ended in Rome. Rome was a flea market of borrowed gods and conquered peoples, a bargain-basement in two tiers – slaves on the one and gods on the other. There were more people, all crammed into the passages of the Coliseum, and all watched. And then, into this tasteless heap of gold and marble, he came, light footed and clothed in light, with his marked

humanity, his deliberate Galilean provincialism, and from that moment there were neither gods nor peoples, there was only one man.' (Boris Pasternak, *Dr Zhivago*)

Who is this Jesus? The gifts tell us:

1. **Gold: Son of God.** You will need to pick your favourite from John 1:13–14, John 8:58 and John 14:9. These are all strong verses to show that the Magi got it right by presenting gold for a king.

2. **Frankincense: Son of Man, Priest.** Jesus is 'God with us' (Matthew 1:23). Jesus comes to be the Man who is also the Priest, offering himself as the sacrifice for our sins.

   Quote: 'He came here as a man with all the limitations of man, the joys as well as the sorrows, the affections as well as the pains. He did not come here to be brave. He came to be tested as a human being, to suffer and to feel pain beyond the power to endure, to be humiliated and to die.' (Jim Bishop, *The Day Christ Died*)

3. **Myrrh: Saviour.** This is the great factor of the uniqueness of Jesus.

   Quote: 'Jesus is not one of the world's great. Talk about Alexander the Great, Charles the Great, Napoleon the Great, if you will: Jesus is apart. He is not only the Great, he is the Only. He is simply Jesus.' (Carnegie Simpson)

   Refer back to Matthew 1:21: the very name 'Jesus' means 'Saviour'. Explain how he wants to be our Saviour today.

   The myrrh for his burial was not the end: he rose again and lives today.

Quote: 'A man may find difficulty in writing a poem, but if he cries, "Oh William Shakespeare, help me!" nothing whatever happens. A man may be terribly afraid, but if he cries, "Oh Horatio Nelson, help me!" there is no sort of reply. But if he is at the end of his moral resources, or cannot by effort of will muster up sufficient positive love and goodness and he cries, "Oh Christ, help me!" something happens at once. The sense of spiritual reinforcement, of drawing spiritual vitality from a living source, is so marked that Christians cannot help being convinced that their Hero is far more than an outstanding figure of the past.' (J. B. Phillips, *Your God Is Too Small*)

Ending: The challenge is whether we will bring the gold, frankincense and myrrh of our lives to worship this Christ, no longer a child, but King of kings.

Quote/Story: Earl Cairns, a great MP and lawyer, when a small boy, had someone say to him, 'God claims you.' He told his mother, who asked him, 'What are you going to do about the claim?' He replied, 'I shall own it and give myself to him.' It was a life-long commitment.

In our hearts we bow down, like the Magi, and worship.

3. January 6: Epiphany

WHEN: Epiphany. Sunday before/after January 6.

WHO: Men.

AIM: To speak of the courage of the Magi, the cost of becoming a Christian and the glory of so doing.

HINT: This is a very well-known incident, so try to make it really come alive. Tell the story from the point of view of the wise men, showing their determination and struggle, with the ultimate triumph. Enthuse throughout!

BIBLE READING: Matthew 2:1–12.

OUTLINE:
Introduction: Sometimes a talk benefits from a dramatic opening statement. Here is one: 'The gate to life is narrow, and the way that leads to it is hard, and there are few people who find it.' Say it with style. Now say that you will prove the truth of these words of Jesus from Matthew 7:14 with the help of some brave men.

   Quote: 'How far is it to Bethlehem? Not very far.' (Children's carol)

You could say that these lovely words are not true for some people. It is hard to become a Christian. The wise men wanted to come to Jesus, but two barriers arose.

Circumstances were hard: Pose the question, 'How long did the journey take?' Query whether it took several months: if not, why did Herod order children under two to be killed, not just babies (2:16)? Jesus is now a 'child' (not a 'baby') in a 'house' (2:11). Speak of the problems of discovering the star and then trying to follow it. Ask if they think the Magi ever felt like giving up.

You could also talk about their ignorance: the Magi did not know of the prophecy in Micah 5:2, quoted in verse 6. Explain how most people come to Jesus knowing very little, but that he will light the way: you could refer to both John 8:12 and Psalm 119:105. Our circumstances are not insurmountable.

> **Quote:** 'Stop talking to God about how big your mountains are; start talking to your mountains about how big your God is.' (David Borgan, Pastor, International Christian Fellowship, Portimâo, Portugal)

People were difficult: Talk about unhelpful Herod (verse 3) and the religious leaders and lawyers with their head knowledge (verse 4). They gave, at best, half-hearted encouragement: so near and yet so far. There was the sting in Herod's instruction (verse 8).

Explain that people are often our problem, too.

> **Quote/Story:** *The Sunday Times* has a quirky column entitled 'Mrs Mills answers all your problems'. One letter was headed 'There are weirdos in my choir'. It read: 'I

recently took on a church choir as choirmaster. It consists mainly of housewives aged between 30 and 60, a few children, four middle-aged men and three men in their twenties. The last group puzzles me: why do they come and sing in a church choir every week when they could go to the cinema or clubs and mix with girls of their own age? They are better-looking than average, they are certainly not paid to come, like myself, nor are they forced to go to the choir by their mothers. What do you think about this?' Mrs Mills, usually flippant and dismissive, replied, 'Have you entertained the bizarre possibility that they are believers? Strange as it may sound, there are some around.'

Tell your hearers not to be put off. The Magi weren't and:

In the end: Jesus: Quote verses 9–11. You could say how, as the Magi fulfilled a prophecy from many hundreds of years before (Isaiah 60:3), so your hearers can come, after 2,000 more years, to acknowledge Jesus as King (gold), the Priest who brings us to God (frankincense) and the One who died for us (myrrh).

Enthuse about how great it was for them and how ultimate it is for us, too.

Ending: On this last day of Christmas:

Quote: 'Christmas is a time for giving, not swapping. It is a time for giving up our sins, giving in to Christ by surrendering our lives, and giving out to others in a true Christian spirit. It is Christmas in the heart that puts Christmas in the air.' (W. T. Ellis)

Say that as we take down our decorations, we, who may have missed the 'story so far', may come at last, like the wise men, to meet Christ – whatever and whoever has stopped us up to now.

4. January 25: Feast of St Paul

WHEN: Feast of the Conversion of St Paul (January 25). Sunday before/after. Pentecost.

WHO: 'Church' people.

AIM: To use this unique event in the church calendar (the only day in the whole year when 'conversion' is specifically mentioned) to answer the knotty question of whether we all need a 'Damascus Road experience', and to encourage our hearers to have their own encounter with Jesus.

BIBLE READING: Acts 22:1–16.

OUTLINE:

Introduction: You could begin by saying how this is a bit of a scary day for many church people, because it is about a very dramatic conversion, and we are worried either that we haven't had anything like this happen to us, or that we might have to! So, let's try and look at this calmly. . .

The Damascus Road: Then: Simply tell the story, briefly, and bring it to life again. Talk of Saul, his good education, his social position (Philippians 3:4–6 helps) and his passionate belief that Christianity was wrong – whereas it was he who was wrong.

Quote: 'A man said to me, "You Christians have been brainwashed." I agreed, but so has everyone. The only difference between us Christians and you is that we chose who washed our brains.' (Barry McGuire, singer, on his album *To the Bride*)

Go on to the journey to Damascus, the light and the question (verse 7), which Saul did not deny. Say how Saul was blinded temporarily, later meeting Ananias and receiving sight, forgiveness and the power of the Holy Spirit.

It would be good to show the value of this in three ways:

1. It was important for Saul. He became Paul, with a wonderfully changed life.

2. It was important for Christianity. Joke about how the New Testament would be half the size without Paul's story and letters! He became the greatest spreader and writer of Christianity ever.

   Quote: 'What happened on the Damascus Road is the most important event in the history of Christianity from Pentecost to our own day.' (Professor F. F. Bruce, former Professor of Biblical Criticism and Exegesis, University of Manchester)

3. It is important for us, because it shows it is possible to meet Jesus after his return to heaven. Say that it means that we can meet Jesus today, leading to:

The Damascus Road: Now: Ask the big question: 'Have you ever had an encounter with Jesus?'

1. **You need to.** Talk about what a 'good' man Paul was, reminding your hearers of what you have shared of his excellent background – a very 'religious' man. But:

Quote: 'I am Jesus – and you are treating me like an enemy.' (Alan Dale's paraphrase of Acts 22:8)

Show how Paul himself talks of his sins needing to be washed away (verse 16). Admit that our problem as 'good church people' is owning up to our wrongs: we are proud people.

Quote: 'God is not out to hurt our pride – he's out to kill it.' (Donald Pfotenhauer)

2. **Jesus wants you to.** The 'light' (verse 6) is the 'light of the world' (John 8:12). Explain that Jesus did not come just to expose our sins with his light, but to die for them on the cross and to rise again to bring us new life. As Paul rose up, so must we. Warn your hearers that Jesus will have plans for them, too (verse 15a).

3. **You can.** State the obvious – this isn't the Damascus Road and your hearers are not called Saul a.k.a Paul. We do not have to ape another's experience. But all our good efforts do not convert us.

Quote: 'I who went to America to convert others, was myself never converted to God.' (John Wesley, shortly before his own conversion, quoted by J. C. Ryle, *Christian Leaders of the Eighteenth Century*)

We need to meet Jesus here – as we are.

Ending:

Quote: 'Not a new start to life, but a new life to start.' (Rob Parsons)

You could use verses 13 and 14 to invite your hearers to meet Jesus, receiving his forgiveness (verse 16) and new life. Consider how you might give an opportunity for them to do that – perhaps time for silent prayer, or an invitation to talk privately afterwards (public confession can always come later!). Or both.

5. February 14: Valentine's Day

WHEN: Valentine's Day. Sunday before/after.

WHO: Young people. Ladies. Non-Christians.

AIM: To show that, whatever the state of our love life, God loves us. This talk therefore fits those who are not in love as well as those who are.

HINT: If you only want one reading, 1 John will do.

BIBLE READINGS: Hosea 14; 1 John 4:7–21.

OUTLINE:

Introduction: Start off by saying how great it is to be in love – sometimes. We all love being loved.

> **Quotes:** 'Who loves ya, baby?' (Telly Savalas, *Kojak*).

> 'There is nothing in the whole world so painful as feeling that one is not liked.' (Sei Shōnagon, Japanese diarist (966–1013), *Pillow Talk*)

Now say you have excellent news: someone loves us and his love will never fade or die – God.

His love in creation: Share the loveliness of Genesis 1: everything God made was 'good'.

Quote: 'Thank you for making me so wonderfully complex! It is amazing to think about. Your workmanship is marvellous and how well I know it.' (Psalm 139:14, The Living Bible)

You could say how we are going to have the opportunity to thank God for this love when we get to heaven, as part of the song there (Revelation 4:11). Ask how we react to this love from God: are we those who don't even believe he did it (Psalm 14:1)? Can we help others to believe in our wonderful creator God?

Quote: 'I want to sow doubts in the minds of the agnostics.' (Garth Hewitt, about his songs)

His love in redemption: You could do worse than use John 3:16 to show that 'God so loved . . . that he gave . . .' The extent of God's love in redeeming us is brilliantly shown in Philippians 2:5–8.

Quote: 'There cannot be a God of love,' men say, 'because, if there were, and he looked upon the world, his heart would break.' The church points to the cross and says, 'It did break.' 'It is God who made the world,' men say, 'so it is he who should bear the load.' The church points to the cross and says, 'He did bear it.' (Archbishop William Temple)

Ask again: How do we react to God's love shown by sending his Son to earth? Speak of how, when Jesus declared God's love when he was here and sought to show that love by righting wrongs, the people of his day put him to death – they refused his love.

Quote: 'Christ cleansed the Temple and, from that moment, the plot to destroy him began. Christ knew it and he faced open-eyed the betrayal and violence, because there was no other way to reveal to rebel man the ghastly tragedy of his sin and the glory and love of God.' (Professor E. M. Blaiklock)

Go to the 1 John reading, using verse 9 and on to verse 10, to show this amazing love.

Quote/Story: James Denny, the Scottish preacher, wanted to go into every pulpit with a crucifix, hold it up and say, 'God loves you like that.'

His love now: Jesus is here, now, to love us.

Quote: 'God was man in Palestine
                 And lives today.'
             (John Betjeman, from his poem 'Christmas')

You could use 1 John 4:16: 'God is love.'

Quote: 'We can say "God is love", yes, not merely has love, but is love.' (J. Denham Smith, *The Gospel in Hosea*)

This (with its source) would take you to the Hosea reading, at verse 4: even if we have never let God love us, he will put things right. His invitation could be the one in Isaiah 1:18. Say that your reason for loving God is in 1 John 4:19. If you also want to show that love can only be given and received if done so freely, use John 1:11–12.

Ending: Ask again, 'Who loves ya?' Give your answer: God does, so receive his love – today.

6. February 14: Valentine's Day

WHEN: Valentine's Day. Sunday before/after.

WHO: Ladies. Non-Christians.

AIM: To show how much God loves us, whether anyone else does or not. It shows how God's love is both the best and for ever.

HINT: This talk is a walk-through of the happy-sad-happy love story of Hosea and Gomer. You will need to read the book first – it won't take long! It will mirror the greatest love story in the world. Although there is a 1 John reading, chapters and verses are all from Hosea, unless otherwise shown.

BIBLE READINGS: Hosea 2:13–23; 1 John 4:7–21.

OUTLINE:
Introduction: Find something light to talk about romance being alive and well – flowers, chocolates, cards and so on. (Maybe have a few on hand as tasty illustrations.) Have a couple in your meeting just got married or announced their engagement?

   Quote: 'Theirs was a love affair pure and simple: she

was pure and he was. . .' (Revd Keith Murray, from the best man's speech at his son's wedding)

Say you are going to look at a happy-sad-happy love affair today, taken from the book of Hosea.

Boy meets girl: Use the nice bits of Hosea 1:2–3: 'Go take a wife . . . so he went and took Gomer . . . and she bore him a son.' Ask your hearers if they remember their first love, so sweet and tender.

> **Quote:** 'That last summer when life still appeared to pay heed to individuals, and when it was easier and more natural to love than to hate.' (Boris Pasternak, *The Last Summer*)

Explain how the story of Hosea is true and historical, but his relationship with Gomer is also a picture of God and his people. Say how God loves each one of us. For some of us, perhaps when we were very small, we loved God in return – talk about childhood bedtime prayers, perhaps a childlike trust in Jesus.

Girl leaves boy: Come to 2:5, using Isaiah 53:6 to show we have done this with God.

> **Quote/Story:** *The Times* carried correspondence on the subject 'What's wrong with the world?' G. K. Chesterton wrote a letter on that subject: 'Dear Sir, I am, Yours faithfully.'

As Gomer left Hosea, so we have gone from God: Revelation 2:4 is good here, as is the story of the prodigal son (Luke 15:11–31). Go to 2:8 (the RSV is better with 'She did not know') to show Hosea's continuing love, and point to God's never-ending love, despite our sin and desertion.

Girl comes back: Tell the story of Gomer sinking to the slave market, with the remarkable 'I bought her' (3:2). Now use 1 John 4:10 to show Jesus paying with his life to win us back so that we could love God again: 1 John 4:19.

  Quote: 'There is no cheap grace.' (Dave Burton)

To emphasise this cost of regaining our love, you could use 1 Peter 1:18–19 and 1 Corinthians 6:19–20. Point out that Jesus is our only hope: 'Beside me there is no Saviour' (Hosea 13:4, RSV). Ask if the love affair between your hearers and God has been restored yet – or is now the time to come back?

A new start: Draw from three great promises in Hosea to show how God makes things right in every area:

1. **Past.** The promise of 14:4 could be linked with 1 John 1:7b. Explain how the death of Jesus means all our sins are washed away.

2. **Present.** The new relationship for Gomer with Hosea is beautifully described in 2:18–20. Use these verses to speak of our wonderful, though completely undeserved, new life in Christ.

3. **Future.** The famous words of 13:14, 'Death, where is your sting, grave where is your victory?', are quoted in this way by Paul (1 Corinthians 15:55): tell your hearers they are the assurance of every Christian.

  Quote: 'I don't want people to stand up at my funeral

service and say what a good person I was – I want them to know I am forgiven.' (Kate Curry, to her husband, Eddie, shortly before her death from cancer, July 2006)

Ending: Use 2:7, 'I will go and return' (RSV), to encourage each hearer to give their love and life to the God who has always loved them.

7. March 19: Feast of St Joseph the Worker

WHEN: Feast of St Joseph. Sunday before/after. Easter Eve. Christmas.

WHO: Men. New Christians.

AIM: To show, by looking at the Gospels' two Josephs, that Christians are brave people who dare to stand up and be counted for Jesus Christ, and that they gain everything by risking everything.

HINT: This is a very multi-purpose talk. Simply adapt it to the occasion. Speak with warmth about these two men, making them come alive as you go through the talk.

BIBLE READINGS: Matthew 1:18–25; Mark 15:42–46.

OUTLINE:
Introduction: Ask, as an opener, 'Have you ever heard the expression "Holy Joe"?' Explain that some Christians used to be called that. Go on to ask if that is what a Christian is – stuck up, 'pious' and goody-goody.

Now say you're going to talk about a couple of guys who were both called Joe, who will show that, even though they were holy and called Joe, they were not Holy Joes! The first was around when Jesus was born, the other when he died: Joseph of Nazareth and Joseph of Arimathea. They will show us what a real Christian is.

A relationship: This is where you take Joseph of Nazareth to show that knowing Jesus is not primarily about rules and regulations, but about a personal relationship with him. The Matthew 1 reading could be told as a great story from Joseph's standpoint: how he was worried, probably embarrassed, the angel telling him not to worry (verse 20), how he was to take Mary home (verse 20) and call her son Jesus (verse 21) – meaning 'Saviour'. And he did (verse 24).

You can agree that there were rules to keep, as in the ritual at eight days (Luke 2:22–24), and he did not always understand Jesus (Luke 2:48). The key point to get across is how Jesus became part of Joseph's life and home: a personal relationship.

> **Quote:** 'All Christian witness will finally be a direct witness, to stand up and be counted or to wear one's heart on one's sleeve unmistakeably for Jesus Christ's sake, confessing him to be Lord and Saviour.' (Robert Short, *The Gospel According to Peanuts*)

'Religion' becomes a relationship, which includes:

A risk: Stick for a moment longer with Joseph of Nazareth: he faced 'public disgrace' (Matthew 1:19) and ended up as a refugee (Matthew 2:14). Admit that there are risks, there is a cost, to being involved with Jesus.

Quote: 'We need to learn a holiness that rejects all compromise with evil and a generosity that seeks and saves the lost.' (Leslie Newbiggin, *Proper Confidence*)

Come to the other Joseph, showing his stand against the vast majority who voted against Jesus (Matthew 26:66). John 19:38 is a good verse, as it shows he had to overcome his fear, while Mark 15:43 demonstrates his great courage, and Matthew 27:60 says it was his own tomb: costly in so many ways. He would not compromise.

Quote: 'Ruthless holiness.' (Luis Palau)

You could compare this with the old meaning of 'Holy Joe', saying that only the brave stand up for Jesus. But you have saved the best until last:

A revelation: 'Christianity is a miracle!' you can say. For Joseph of Nazareth, the Saviour of the world came into his home and life.

For Joseph of Arimathea, say that it was his stone which was rolled away (Mark 16:4): Jesus rose from his grave (Mark 16:6). This 'Holy Joe' wants us to know we can have forgiveness and a new, eternal life. It's all true.

Quote: 'The greatest miracle that God can perform today is to take an unholy man out of an unholy world, and make that man holy, and put him back into the unholy world and keep him holy in it.' (Leonard Ravenhill)

Ending: Enthuse your hearers to be Holy Joes in the way these Josephs were, with Jesus in their hearts and homes, however hard it may be.

Quote: 'A holy man is an awesome weapon in God's hands.' (Robert Murray McCheyne)

8. March 25: The Annunciation

WHEN: Feast of the Annunciation to the Blessed Virgin Mary. Sunday before/after. Mothering Sunday.

AIM: Many talks on the annunciation look at the messenger (Gabriel) or the recipient (Mary). For a change, this talk looks at the message – the annunciation itself – and aims to put across something of the unique greatness of this very special day.

HINT: With your subject being the greatest announcement in the history of the world, try to convey something of the wonder and excitement: a little passion would not go amiss. The verses are from the Luke reading, unless stated otherwise.

BIBLE READINGS: Isaiah 11:1–9; Luke 1:26–38.

OUTLINE:
Introduction: Start by saying how clever speakers are at making simple things sound complicated. Today, you will attempt the reverse – to try to make a mystery understandable. Tell your hearers you are, of course, referring to the annunciation which, to simplify, means 'announcing' or, we might say, 'And introducing. . .'

Announcing – who? Tell the story, briefly, of Gabriel, God's messenger (verse 26), coming to Mary (verse 27) with the amazing news that she would be the mother of a unique baby. Who would this be? Here are your descriptions of the coming One, the 'and introducing. . .'.

- **Jesus** (verse 31). Say that, for us, this is the first and most important description, because without this nothing can follow. Explain the meaning of the word, looking at Matthew 1:21 – 'Saviour'. Ask your hearers if they have any sins. Then this one is for them.

- **Son of God** (verses 32 and 35). Isaiah 11:2 comes in here, as does Matthew 1:23. Show that this is the obvious reason why God had to be his Father – hence a 'virgin birth' (Isaiah 7:14). You told them you'd keep it simple! Speak of the wonder of God coming to us in this way.

- **King** (verse 33). Join Isaiah 11:1 with verse 32, but show that, compared with King David, Jesus' reign will never end (verse 33).

Quotes: 'History is His story.' (Val Grieve)

'The hinge of history is on the door of a Bethlehem stable.' (Ralph Sockman)

- **Holy One** (verse 35). Speak of Jesus coming in the power of the Holy Spirit as 'the Holy One'. Urge your hearers never to treat Jesus lightly: he is ultimately special. Explain that it is because Jesus is who he is that we can have our own right relationship with God.

Quote: 'God doth justify the believing man, yet not for the worthiness of his belief, but for his worthiness who is believed.' (Richard Hooker, 1593)

It would be good to bring in Isaiah 11:4–5, to show a holy rule of justice: admit that we like the nice bits about Jesus, but some of this is harder to accept – however, it is all true.

> **Quote:** 'Fear him, ye saints, and you will then
> Have nothing else to fear.'
> (Nahum Tate and Nicholas Brady, from the hymn 'Through All the Changing Scenes of Life')

Coming – how?

- **Born of Mary** (verses 31 and 35). Show that, because of Mary's willingness (verse 38), Jesus comes from his glorious heaven to be a real human being, to bring God down to us.

  Quote: 'In worldly advancement a man climbs up rung by rung in honour and prestige and power. But Jesus climbed rung by rung downward, and still he climbed.'
  (Søren Kierkegaard)

- **By the Holy Spirit** (verse 35). Speak of God doing this miracle to get Jesus here as our Saviour.

Ending: Verse 37 is lovely because it enables you to 'announce' that this Jesus can now come to us, by his Spirit, to live in us for ever.

9. Mother's Day

WHEN: Mothering Sunday. Family service.

WHO: Parents.

AIM: To show that our families are to be there for God, as God is there for our families.

HINT: These are days when family life is at a premium, so give this talk positively, generously and enthusiastically.

BIBLE READINGS: Colossians 3:18–21; Ephesians 5:22 – 6:4.

OUTLINE:
Introduction: Here is a good one!

> **Quote:** The British Council, in November 2004, surveyed 35,000 people in all non-English speaking countries for the most beautiful words in the English language. Giggle was at 45, Lullaby 26, with the top ten: 10 Tranquillity, 9 Liberty, 8 Freedom, 7 Destiny, 6 Fantastic, 5 Eternity, 4 Love, 3 Smile, 2 Passion and at Number 1 – Mother.

Now say that, today, you are sharing how important families are, especially mothers. Quote Exodus 20:12.

Families have God's construction: Show how, from the beginning, God planned marriage – use Genesis 2:24 and 1:28.

From the Ephesians reading, show that families mirror God's relationship with his people (verse 25). Say that God has built us to live in families. You could comment on how, in Africa and Asia especially, they have 'extended families' compared with our small units. But –

> **Quote:** 'We don't have an extended family: you have an impoverished family.' (Said by an Indian to Olive Drane)

You may want to speak of the value of families: be sure not to hurt singles, single parents and adopted children. For the latter, the following is good:

> **Quote:** 'I grew in mummy's heart, not in her tummy.' (A little girl, about her adoption)

Families have God's conditions: Bring in Exodus 20:12 again and then you could simply read the very short Colossians reading, showing there is no room for male chauvinism or women's lib. Speak especially of a husband's love, from Ephesians 5:25–28, showing how Jesus washed the disciples' feet and died on a cross. Do men love like that?

If you talk about children, the Good News Bible has 'respect' in Exodus 20:12, and the balance is nicely shown in Ephesians 6:4. Ask if we parents are playing our part, not annoying our children, but bringing them up to love Jesus. There may be nudges exchanged if families are sitting together – you could even jokingly comment about this. Proverbs 22:6 is a good promise to use here.

Quote/Story: Ruth Graham, evangelist Billy Graham's wife, was asked why her teenage sons behaved badly. She replied: 'It says, "Train up a child in the way he should go, and when he is old he will not turn from it." It does not say, "Train up a child in the way he should go, and when he is a teenager he will not depart from it"!'

Families have God's concern: Back to Ephesians 6:2–3, to show that Exodus 20:12 is the one Commandment with a promise. God promises a good life if we let our families be his family, too. Show how we can all know God as 'our Father' (Matthew 6:9). Point to the fact that God loves us all and wants to bless our homes and our families today.

Ending: Even though some of it sounds a bit old-fashioned, here is a prayer for families to pray together in church. You could use it (amended, if you wish):

Quote: 'Lord, behold our family here assembled. We thank thee for this place in which we worship; for the love that unites us, for the peace accorded us this day, for the hope with which we expect the morrow, for the health, the work, the food, and the bright skies that make our lives delightful; for our friends in all parts of the earth.

'Give us courage and gaiety and the quiet mind. Bless us, if it may be, in all our innocent endeavours. And, if it may not, give us strength to encounter that which is to come, that we be brave in peril, temperate in wrath and, in all the changes of fortune and down to the gates of death, loyal and loving to one another.

'As the clay to the potter, as the windmill to the wind, as the children to their father, we beseech thee of this help and mercy, for Christ's sake, Amen.' (Robert Louis Stevenson)

10. Mother's Day

WHEN: Mother's Day. Family service.

WHO: Children. Parents.

AIM: To show God's love for mothers (parents) and children. To encourage each hearer to let God love them, because he wants to.

ACTIVITY: This talk is based on a great verse: why not get everyone to learn it? It does work! Lead them through it, phrase by phrase, repeating it after you. Next time do the whole thing – including where the verse comes from: 'Cast all your worries on God, because he cares for you' (1 Peter 5:7, author's paraphrase).

BIBLE READING: Genesis 21:8–21 (for children).

OUTLINE:
Introduction: Say how you have a lovely prayer and you want to prove it is true:

> **Quote:** 'God who made the grass,
> The flower, the fruit, the tree,
> The day and night to pass,
> Cares for me.'
> (*The Lion Book of Children's Prayers*)

This is true for grown-ups and for children. You have two stories you want to tell them.

For grown-ups: This talk is about Hagar and Ishmael from Genesis 16 (the whole chapter) and Genesis 21. Because you will not want two long readings, tell the story of Genesis 16 here without reading it out.

You could do it as a 'Once upon a time, long ago. . .' as long as you say this is a true story. First, tell the story of Hagar from Genesis 16 – a used and abused slave, forced to have a baby by a man who did not love her. Alas, she was not perfect herself, boasting to her mistress, then driven away.

A hopeless case? Speak of how we often feel like used, unloved 'nobodies'. But God was there for her (16:7). 'Ishmael' means 'God hears'. God loves us grown-ups when no one else does.

For children: Here is the second story, about an unloved child. This slave-boy Ishmael is not wanted at home. Tell the story of him and his mother, Hagar, being sent away. Make it dramatic – bring it to life! Get them out in the desert, helpless and hopeless, with Ishmael put under a tree to die (21:15–16).

Quote: 'Nobody likes me, everybody hates me,
          I'm going down the garden to eat worms:
          Long thin slimy ones, short fat fuzzy ones,
          Gooey, gooey, gooey, gooey worms.'
          (Anon)

Say that we all feel like that sometimes! Then come to the drama of 21:17. Who cared? Not Ishmael's father, who sent him away. Not his mother, who left him to die. Yes – she prayed, but whose voice did God hear?

Make it really count as you tell your hearers that God loves them, is listening to them, hears them. He provided for Ishmael (21:19) and will for us. Yes, Ishmael's life was hard: 21:20 shows this. But God was there into his adult life.

Ending: You could end as you began. Get your hearers to see if they can remember the sentence they learned at the beginning – say it together a couple of times. Then turn it into a prayer of thanks for and response to God's love and care.

11. Mother's Day

WHEN: Mother's Day. Family service.

WHO: Ladies. Older people.

AIM: To show the value and cost of allowing Jesus to be part of our homes and lives.

HINT: Although this talk praises a mother, it also speaks of all who would use their homes for God and can be a challenge to men and women to have homes which honour Jesus Christ.

BIBLE READING: Mark 2:1–12.

OUTLINE:

Introduction: Can you think of a give-away line? Think of something you have heard someone say which revealed a secret about them: for example, how they gave their age away by remembering an incident like the Coronation (so they had to be at least so old. . .).

There is a give-away line in Mark 2:1. Jesus had 'come home'. But he didn't have a home, did he? If he did, wasn't it in Nazareth? Now check Matthew 4:13, which confirms this verse. With whom had Jesus made his home? Go back to Mark 1:29–31. Speak of this incident with warmth, bringing it alive again as you talk of a sick mother being healed as she and Jesus meet. The end of verse 31 shows what she did: she welcomed Jesus to her home.

Your home? Ask the question: 'Have you ever let Jesus come and share your home?' Peter's mother-in-law did, because of the love and care he had shown her and her family.

Look at all the wonderful things Jesus does for us! You could speak of his forgiveness, his concern for us as individuals, his new life, his willingness to welcome us to his home in heaven. Surely we can do no other than return the compliment?

> **Quote:** 'Home is the place where, when you have to go there, they have to take you in.' (Robert Frost, American poet, 'The Death of the Hired Man')

Say how amazing it is that the great Son of God would live with us. Everyone will come to know this. The RSV has, 'It was reported that he was at home' in 2:1; the GNB, 'The news spread that he was at home'. Laugh about how people will gossip!

The up-side: Tell your hearers about the blessings Jesus brought: the mother-in-law healed, going on to 1:32–34. The neighbours and friends got in on the goodness of Jesus. Ask whether we are to hug the good things from God to ourselves, or share them. How wonderful if our homes were to be used as places where people came to receive forgiveness and new life.

Quote: 'Who bestows himself with alms feeds three,
Himself, his hungering neighbour, and Me.'
(Lowell, from 'The Vision of Sir Launfal',
quoted by Thomas Hughes in *Tom Brown's
Schooldays*).

The down-side: Tell the story, briefly, of 2:1–11 from the
point of view of the mother-in-law. Do it with humour,
speaking of her loss of privacy as everyone invaded her
home to hear her house-guest and the horror of seeing her
roof ripped open (2:4). Not everyone was friendly (2:6–7)
but more blessings flowed (2:12).

It's not always easy to have Jesus around.

Out or in? You could refer to the tragedy of John 1:11 –
the closed home. Yet there is the 'God-shaped hole' without
Jesus.

Quote: 'You awake us to delight in your praise; for you
made us for yourself and our heart is restless till it rests in
you.' (Augustine, *Confessions*)

Who, of your hearers, will let Jesus into their home today?

Quote: 'The holy door we have to open is the door of
our hearts.' (Archbishop Derek Warlock, former Roman
Catholic Archbishop of Liverpool, in his Pastoral Letter,
Lent 1983)

The beautiful picture of Jesus in Revelation 3:20 would
make a lovely ending, with a prayer for response.

12. Lent

WHEN: Lent.

WHO: Non-Christians. Prisoners.

AIM: As Lent is a time for acknowledging our shortcomings and for seeking God's way, this talk aims to help these to happen.

HINT: There is a lot in this talk based on Psalm 40. Keep it moving.

BIBLE READING: Psalm 40:1–11.

OUTLINE:

Introduction: If you are giving this talk in Lent, an honest opening would work, along the lines of, 'Lent is a very special time, when we try to get our lives back on a spiritual track. The good news is – we're not the first. King David did it long ago – let's see how.' If it is not Lent, you can say this is something we all need to do from time to time. Here are the stages.

The sin: The picture language of verse 2 is great for speakers: draw from it in the different translations to show the mess we all get into:

- Sin takes us away from God: 'A lonesome pit' (Moffat), 'the desolate pit' (RSV). Talk of the tragedy of life without God.
- Sin soils and spoils our lives: 'the miry clay' (Jerusalem Bible), 'the slimy pit' (NIV), 'an horrible pit' (KJV). We get in a mess.

Quote: 'What a lamentable thing it is that men should blame the gods and regard us as the source of their troubles, when it is their own wickedness that brings them sufferings worse than any which Destiny allots them.' (Zeus in Homer, *The Odyssey*)

- Sin kills: 'The deadly pit' (Jerusalem Bible). We may even refuse God's help:

Quote: 'Jesus died for somebody's sins but not mine.' (Patti Smith, from the song 'Gloria')

You could bring in verse 6 here: our own good efforts are not the answer to our sin.

The Saviour: Use verses 6–8, as 'lifted' by Hebrews 10:5–9, to show how Jesus is the one who comes to our rescue, as our substitute.

Quote: 'Justification means this miracle: that Christ takes our place and we take his.' (Emil Brunner, quoted by John Stott in *The Cross of Christ*)

Yet another Bible version has 'Lord, you save us' – Good News Bible, verse 9. Ask your hearers if they are relying on themselves, or on what Jesus has done on the cross.

The saving: As last, verse 1: we wait, we cry and the Lord pulls us out (verse 2) as we trust him (verse 4).

> **Quote:** 'Christ's call is to the individual. There is no substitute for the individual's response to Jesus Christ.' (Robin Eames, former Archbishop of Armagh)

You could use the difference between a rope being lowered to us from a helicopter as we drown in the sea and us failing to grab it, and a lifeboat rescue where we are pulled in and sail home safely.

The sharing: Draw from verse 3 to show how this wonderful news is not to be held selfishly, but given to others. All of us can and must share the news with others.

> **Quote:** 'When a young man I know joined a church, the preacher asked him, "What was it I said that induced you to be a Christian?" He replied, "It was nothing I ever heard you say – it was the way my mother lived." ' (Billy Sunday)

The supplying: If you have time, the following could show God's ongoing help:

- Protection (verse 2): the safety God gives.
- Provision (verses 5 and 11): God looking after us.
- Prosperity (verses 5 and 10): God's guidance.
- Presence (verses 10 and 11): God's love is always there.

Ending: As the word 'Lent' comes from an Old English word meaning 'spring', you could end by saying that God wants to bring us from the winter of our old life to new life in him, giving us a fresh start: why not take it?

13. Lent

WHEN: Lent. Good Friday. Communion/Eucharist.

AIM: To show how vital the cross of Christ is to our corporate and personal lives as Christians.

HINT: It would be easy to play down other aspects of the Christian faith in giving this talk: try to be positive as you enthuse about the cross.

BIBLE READING: Galatians 6:11–18.

OUTLINE:

Introduction: Talk about the fact that Paul wrote a large part of the New Testament and then ask, 'How many verses did he write with his own hand?' The remarkable answer is 15, of which over half are in our reading. Now ask, 'What is it here that is so important that he makes it extra-personal?' Answer: he brings us to the very centre of our faith.

>   **Quote:** 'We live in an age of disillusionment; we need, not new illusions, but ancient realities.' (*The Daily Telegraph*, leader, 3.4.80)

The centre: Start with verse 14 and ask whether this is a statement we would make, both as a church and individually. You could also ask, 'Where is the cross in our theology?'

> **Quote:** 'I simply argue that the cross be raised again at the centre of the market place as well as on the steeple of the church.' (George McLeod)

It may be a little controversial to say this – because people speak of Paul's brilliant reasoning at Athens – but you could say how the Acts 17:16–34 sermon led to a small response, with the cross never mentioned. Show how, in the next verse (Acts 18:1), Paul went to Corinth, where he only preached about the cross – as he says to them in 1 Corinthians 2:2 – leading to an amazing church being formed. Ask if this was the turning point in Paul's ministry – and his life: bring in Galatians 2:20.

> **Quote:** 'The call of the cross is to enter into the passion of Christ. We must have upon us the print of the nails.' (Gordon Watt)

Challenge your hearers to let their lives and their message be cross-centred.

The edge: The next challenge is to ask if your hearers have moved to the edge, as the Galatians had, relying on ritual, emphasising outward show and keeping the law. The message of the cross is especially vital if we are relying on what we ourselves do.

> **Quote:** 'The proclamation proves necessary for innumerable people who have been baptized but who live

quite outside the Christian life.' (Pope Paul VI, *Evangelii Nuntiandi*)

Ask if we allow the cross to be sidelined in the songs we sing and whether we emphasise other things too much. Show how, at the centre of heaven, is 'the Lamb who was slain' (Revelation 5:12), and how John the Baptist pointed to Jesus, not as a reformer, teacher or healer, but as 'the Lamb of God' (John 1:29).

Take your hearers to 1 Corinthians 1:18 to show that our power emanates from the cross.

The heart:

Quote: 'In the cross of Christ I glory,
Towering o'er the wrecks of time.'
(John Bowering)

Bring your hearers to Galatians 6:11–18 to show the wonderful result of bringing the cross to the heart of our lives – verse 16. Take the end of verse 15 – we are then 'a new creation'. Agree that verse 17 shows we cannot escape hardship if we do, bringing in the distancing from wrongdoing (verse 14).

Ending: If you are able to, say that you would wish your own credo to be Paul's in verse 14, asking if your hearers would wish the same.

14. Palm Sunday

WHEN: Palm Sunday.

AIM: To show how we are to be Christians wherever we are and whatever the circumstances.

EXPLANATION: This talk is based on the Luke account of the entry into Jerusalem, the verses below being from there (unless otherwise shown). It shows how Jesus behaved on this famous day, to encourage us to act similarly.

BIBLE READING: Luke 19:28–44.

OUTLINE:

Introduction: Start by talking about the different areas within which we live our lives: sometimes 'up front' (like you, now); sometimes all alone; at other times somewhere in between. Now say how Palm Sunday had these three elements for Jesus, and he can show us, on this Palm Sunday, how to get things right in whichever kind of situation we find ourselves.

In the background: Point out that the dramatic events of Palm Sunday don't start with palm branches. Someone had worked out where the donkey was coming from, made sure it was OK to borrow it, fixed the password. Who? Jesus. The success of the day depended on his private acts.

Quote: 'Every Christian should be an identical twin – identical before God and before man.' (Alec Motyer)

Ask your hearers if we are only Christians when we are 'on show', pointing out that most of being a Christian is far from glamorous. Show how Jesus was great when no one saw. You could ask your hearers if they have a good, personal, private relationship with Jesus.

In the foreground: Now come to the reading – make it come alive and convey the excitement. How thrilling to be with Jesus then – and now.

Quote: 'Of all the people in the Bible, Jesus is the one you'd most like to invite to tea, because you'd have such a good time.' (J. D. Salinger, author of *Catcher in the Rye*, quoted by Tony Robinson on TV, Easter 1995)

Come to verses 37 and 38, showing how God gets the praise and glory. You could cross-reference Matthew 21:5 – which itself draws from Zechariah 9:9 – to show the humanity of Jesus. He brings glory to his Father at his moment of triumph. Ask if we do that – or do we take the credit for our lives?

Quote/Story: Leonardo da Vinci painted his famous fresco of the Last Supper in the Church of St Maria delle Grazie, Milan. A friend of his, entranced by two lovely silver cups on the table in front of Jesus, exclaimed at the artistic skill in their design. The artist took a brush and painted them out: 'It is not that I want you to see – it is that Face.'

A further point here could be how Jesus understood the people's praise and delight and encouraged it (verse 40), despite the 'religious' opposition (verse 39). You could ask if we are boring critics or encouragers of those who enthuse in God.

On the sidelines: This is the in-between bit – not exactly private or public. Bring your hearers to the most poignant part of the day, from verse 41 onwards. Describe the graphic 'weeping over Jerusalem', when Jesus should have been bitter at their rejecting him.

> **Quote:** 'Mercy is God not giving us what we do deserve; grace is God giving us what we do not deserve.' (Anon)

Ask whether we treat people like that, especially those who oppose us. Jesus went on to die for them.

> **Quote:** 'It is one of our greatest tragedies that the church is often more exclusive than God.' (A. B. Davidson)

Ending: Say how Palm Sunday is an object lesson and challenge to us all: Jesus got his attitude and approach just right. Ask if we will learn from him.

15. Maundy Thursday

WHEN: Maundy Thursday. Lent. Sundays after Easter. Feast of St Peter (June 29).

WHO: Christians. Church leaders.

AIM: To take the failings of Peter, on the evening Jesus was betrayed, as a warning to us all – even the key leaders in the church – and to show how Jesus had a grip on the situation, even as Peter was getting it wrong. This should then give hope to us all.

HINT: The restoration of Peter is dealt with more fully in talk 19, which gives a different emphasis. Here, the concentration is on what went wrong, with the part Jesus played in the rescue also being prominent. Note how each section has four points: Peter's four mistakes, Jesus' four answers. The verses are all from Luke (unless stated otherwise).

BIBLE READING: Luke 22:54–62.

OUTLINE:
Introduction: With a smile, say, 'We all make mistakes!' Point out that some mistakes get more publicity than others. The night before Jesus died, one man made some of the most publicised mistakes ever.

Getting it wrong: Simon Peter is our sort-of-hero, who got four things wrong:

1. **He followed in his own strength.** Show how Jesus gave him fair warning (22:31–34).

   Quote: 'Jesus expects us to make mistakes.' (Colin Buckland)

   Compare the answer of Peter in 22:33 with the expanded version in Mark 14:29 and 31: a lot of 'I' shows his self-confidence, not relying on Jesus. Tell your hearers how easy it is for us to be a do-it-yourself Christian (e.g. how often we say the Lord's Prayer without thinking).

   Quotes: 'The Christian is never a self-made man.' (William Lane, *Scripture Union Bible Study Books – Ephesians to 2 Thessalonians*)

   'All growth is Jesus-centred.' (Peter Street)

2. **He followed 'at a distance'** (22:54). Admit that any of us can 'drift', so we visit church rather than worship, read the Bible rather than feed on it, hardly realising we are keeping God at arm's length. Talk about how small children hold onto an adult's hand crossing the road, whereas, when we get older, we do it ourselves.

   Quote: 'The trouble with grown-ups is they can be too sensible for their own good.' (Oliver Howarth)

3. **He followed with the enemies** (22:55). Say how it is sometimes easier not to be too involved as a Christian, especially when everyone else is not exactly acting or

speaking in a Christian way. Jesus is Lord – but not all the time, it seems. . .

4. **He followed too late** (22:56–60). Give the three denials, all so silly and tragic. Share 22:62 as a truly sad verse. Admit that we do fail. Sin and temptation do beat us. We fail to live as God wants us to – even as we want to.

Getting it right: Now for the good news! Jesus can sort it out. He does four positive things to eliminate Peter's negatives.

1. **Jesus looked** (22:60). Point out how Jesus did not turn from Peter when Peter had turned away from Jesus; nor does he turn from us.

   Quote: 'In falling and rising we are always held close in the love of God.' (Julian of Norwich)

2. **Jesus loved.** You could say how, if you had been Jesus, you might have thought, 'Blow this! If my close friend can't stand with me, why should I bother?' But off he went to die – for Peter and us all (c.f. Paul's comment in Galatians 2:20). No wonder Peter wrote as he did in 1 Peter 1:18–19.

3. **Jesus lifted.**

   Quote: 'Dear God, help me to get up. I can fall down by myself.' (Anon)

   He and Peter had a private chat (24:34) and they had their famous post-resurrection meeting (John 21:15–19) when all was put right.

Quote: 'Live as forgiven men.' (Christopher Chevasse, former Bishop of Rochester)

Ask if we let Jesus restore us.

4. **Jesus led.** The John 21 encounter shows Jesus giving Peter a new work to do. Ask if your hearers will go on from here with Jesus.

Ending: Ask your hearers if they spotted the difference. DIY Christianity is a recipe for disaster. Call in the expert to fix things!

16. Good Friday

WHEN: Any time in Lent, especially Good Friday.

WHO: Those whose lives are in a mess. Prisoners.

AIM: To show that, because of the death of Jesus on the cross, we've all got a chance – if only we'll take it. To help us realise it is all down to Jesus and his love, not us. Good news for bad people, tough on the 'goodies'.

HINTS: You don't have to use all six headings (all beginning with the same letter) – pick the points which are needed by your hearers. It is worth reading the accounts in Matthew 27:38–44 and Mark 15:27–32 to discover the full story.

BIBLE READING: Luke 23:32–43.

> **Quote:** 'These verses we have now read deserve to be printed in letters of gold. Multitudes will thank God to all eternity that the Bible contains this story of the penitent thief.' (Bishop J. C. Ryle, 'Expository Thoughts on the Gospels')

OUTLINE: All about the 'penitent thief':

1. **His requirement.** A 'criminal' (verse 32), a 'robber' (Matthew 27:38) who 'reviled' Jesus (Mark 15:32). We are 'criminals', as we break God's law, robbing God of his right to be Number One, getting our lives wrong.

2. **His realisation.** He's getting what he deserves (verse 41), needing Jesus to 'remember' him (verse 42). Do we realise (especially on Good Friday) that we need Jesus? Because:

   Quote: 'There was no other good enough.' (C. F. Alexander, from the hymn 'There is a Green Hill')

3. **His remedy.** 'Jesus' (verse 42): the one who 'has done nothing wrong' (verse 41). Matthew 1:21 is the key. He has no help, or hope, anywhere else. The remedy is for now and the future, into the 'kingdom' (verse 42).

4. **His response.** Verse 42. He pleads nothing:

   Quote: 'Just as I am, without one plea.' (Hymn by Charlotte Elliott, 1834)

   He says he 'fears God' (verse 40), as he turns from his wrong to the Saviour who is dying to pay for it. His response is very public, no doubt ridiculed by his fellow criminal. This point is vital with a tough audience and especially in prison: it is an act of courage.

5. **His receipt.** Verse 43 – the reply of Jesus. He receives total forgiveness and acceptance: refer to Hebrews 7:25, 'Jesus is able to save completely those who come to God through him'.

Quote: 'Some may perchance, with strange surprise,
Have blundered into Paradise.'
(Francis Thompson, from his poem 'Judgement
in Heaven', 1913)

6. **His request.** Verse 40 is a question to us all.

Quotes: 'One thief was saved, that no sinner might
despair; but only one, that no sinner may presume.'
(Anon)

'Eternity is a long time to spend in the wrong place.'
(Flying Pickets, *Live at the Albany Empire* album)

Ending:

Quote: 'Like the thief I cry to thee,
"Remember me". . .
Have mercy on me, O God,
Have mercy on me.'
(Andrew of Crete, AD 660–740)

The dying thief came in time. See 2 Corinthians 6:2: now is
'the day of salvation'.

17. Good Friday

WHEN: Good Friday. Lent. 'Tricky Questions' session.

AIM: To explain the meaning of the cross, answering the hard question, 'Why did Christ have to die?'

HINT: There is quite a lot of ground covered here, so keep the talk going.

BIBLE READING: Isaiah 52:13 – 53:12.

OUTLINE:

Introduction: In Scotland, in the seventeenth century, a remarkable group of Christians known as 'The Covenanters' stood together against much opposition to preserve a purity of faith.

> **Quote:** Their central themes were 'the majesty of God, the loveliness of Christ and the sins and sorrows of the human heart'. (Robert Woodrow, quoted by Alexander Smellie, *Men of the Covenant*)

These three themes give you your outline:

The majesty of God: Three characteristics are vital here:

1. **God is a God of power.** You could use Genesis 1:1, the start of the Ten Commandments (Exodus 20:2) and Psalm 24:10.

   Quote: 'God is God – he does things his way. We must not tie him down.' (Revd Rod Allon-Smith)

2. **God is a God of holiness.** As the reading is from Isaiah, you could use Isaiah 6:3 or 40:25. The future agrees: Revelation 4:8.

3. **God is a God of love.** 1 John 4:16 puts it even stronger: 'is'. If you use Hosea 11:1 as an example of God's love, it will give a good contrast under the next heading.

You need to comment on all three of the above very positively because of the contrasts in what now follows, the third of the Covenanters' themes:

The sins and sorrows of the human heart: We have:

1. **Rebelled against God's power.** Daniel 9:9–10 is helpful here, as is Isaiah 53:6a (from the reading).

2. **Sinned against God's holiness.** Keeping in Isaiah, 64:6 is a sobering verse. Even those who are committed to Christian work sometimes fail here.

   Quote: 'Many a Christian worker has buried his spirituality in the grave of his activity.' (Duncan Campbell, *The Price and Power of Revival*)

3. Trampled on God's love. If you used Hosea, the next verse (Hosea 11:2) is a sad picture of us all. We have spurned God's outstretched hand of love.

Half-way dilemma:

1. Power cannot be compromised or there is chaos: God is not for changing (James 1:17).

2. Holiness cannot be compromised or there is dirt (Habakkuk 1:13). You could contrast clean and dirty bowls of water: what happens if they mix?
The result? We are separated from God: Isaiah 59:2.

3. Love can, however, love on: John 3:16.

Quote: 'God's priority is not for rebuke, but for rescue.' (Revd Peter Findley)

Thank God for the Covenanters' second theme:

The loveliness of Christ: Here comes Jesus, to solve the dilemma. Continue the three headings:

1. Jesus demonstrated God's power: Mark 1:22, with Peter's words in Acts 2:22.
2. He lived a life of holiness: Hebrews 4:15.
3. Concentrate on his love: Matthew 9:36 is lovely.

Why the cross? You can use the meaning of the name 'Jesus' (Matthew 1:21), or Paul's stirring words in 2 Corinthians 5:21.

Quote: 'There was no other good enough
        To pay the price of sin.
        He only could. . .'
        (C. F. Alexander, from the hymn 'There is a
        Green Hill')

The most remarkable comment is in Isaiah 53:10. Jesus took all the results of sin:

- Physical: Isaiah 52:14. He died.
- Mental: Isaiah 53:3.
- Spiritual: separation from God – Matthew 27:46.

What the cross does:

1. It pays for sin (1 John 2:2). Hence the cry 'Finished' (John 19:30) – the Greek *tetelestai* means 'paid for'.

2. It purchases from sin (Acts 20:28).

> **Quote:** 'We need our bishops to tell us, without ambiguity, that there is only one return from our exiled condition, and that is the way of the cross.' (*The Daily Telegraph*, leader, April 1980)

3. It purifies from sin (Hebrews 1:3).

Ending: You could do far worse than use this:

Quote: 'Love so amazing, so divine,
Demands my soul, my life, my all.'
(Isaac Watts, from the hymn 'When I Survey
the Wondrous Cross')

We can come to the foot of the cross – and meet the risen
Christ.

18. Easter

WHEN: Easter. Easter season.

AIM: To show how, at Easter, we can be in danger of nearly meeting Jesus but not quite. But your hearers can get there!

HINT: This talk begins with a personal story. Use it about the author of this book but if you have one of your own, all the better!

BIBLE READING: John 20:10–18.

OUTLINE:

Introductory story: With everyone else's quotes and stories, here is mine! I was having a bonfire in my mother-in-law Joyce's front garden, dressed in my scruffy gardening clothes and flat cap. A woman arrived in her car with a present for my mother-in-law's birthday the next day. I went to her car window. We talked about Joyce not being in: yes, I would give her the gift. I left her to write the card and we talked again before she left. The next day she phoned Joyce with a 'Happy Birthday' and was amazed to hear I was her son-in-law. She knew my voice – she had heard many of my radio broadcasts. She had seen me at my father-in-law's recent funeral, heard me preach, met me then. But, that morning, she thought I was the gardener and had not made the connection. . .

You should be into the talk now, so simply pick up with Mary: what was wrong?

She had the wrong perspective: It would help if you wore glasses! Talk about you (or your partner/parent/whoever) not being able to read the letters on the eye test chart: they were blurred. Go to Mary, crying (verse 11). Her tears blurred her vision. Ask what blurs our vision of Jesus. You could talk about our hurts, bereavements, pain, disbelief and sin, commenting briefly on each one. Do we even make Jesus have tears over some of these?

> **Quote:** 'Jesus weeps over a church that has forgotten the power of the Resurrection.' (Alan Cartwright)

Refer back to the crucifixion to show how Jesus has taken all these 'blurs' on the cross so that we can see.

It was the wrong place: Still in verse 11, speak of Mary looking 'into the tomb'. That's where she expected Jesus to be: not outside.

> **Quote:** 'In all the tragic dramas of antiquity, whether lived or staged, we detect the same pattern: the hero, be he Alexander or Oedipus, reaches his pinnacle only to be cut down. Only in the drama of Jesus does the opposite pattern hold: the hero is cut down, only to be raised up.' (Thomas Cahill, quoted by Philip Yancey, *Reaching for the Invisible God*)

Ask where we expect to meet Jesus: only in church, or in

our past? But what about at home, in the street, in the garden? He may be where we least expect him.

He was the wrong person: Ask what sort of person we expect Jesus to be: are we confused by childhood images?

> **Quote:** 'Gentle Jesus, meek and mild'. (Charles Wesley, hymn)

You could refer back to my (or your) story of not being recognised: the woman expected me to be in suit, collar and tie. Compare with Mary (verse 15) expecting the opposite – 'the gardener'. Say that Jesus is the risen Saviour and Lord. Go on to the very personal way Jesus greeted 'Mary' (verse 16) and how we can have this intimate, personal relationship.

> **Quote:** 'I am a witness to the fact that the Lord Jesus is alive, that he is a person and, though invisible, accessible. I have been cultivating personal acquaintance with a personal Saviour for more than 43 years.' (Bishop Taylor)

Ending: Say how the risen Jesus is with us here, right now. We can meet him and go home with Mary's wonderful words (verse 18) on our lips.

19. Easter

WHEN: Easter. Easter season. Good Friday. Feast of St Peter (June 29).

AIM: To take the famous story of the apostle Peter's dramatic fall from grace and subsequent restoration, to demonstrate how we too may be rescued by Jesus from the mistakes we make as we seek to be his disciples.

HINT: Because this is mainly an Easter talk, only the introduction deals with Peter getting it wrong, although his failures are hinted at as the talk progresses.

BIBLE READING: John 21:15–19.

OUTLINE:

Introduction: A good 'way in' would be to say that the resurrection is about people meeting Jesus. So – what is it like to meet Jesus? Go on to say how there was one extra-special meeting, between Jesus and his disciple, Simon Peter. Explain, briefly, how he had denied Jesus so badly that he probably wondered if he could ever get back again. You could paint the picture of the fishing expedition and subsequent breakfast in John 21:1–14, leading to the one-to-one chat.

For Peter, meeting Jesus meant several 'Ss':

Surrender: Go through a couple of things it doesn't mean. Jesus does not ask Peter if he believes in him, or if he understands. He asks for his love (verse 15). Ask your hearers if they have ever come to love Jesus. You could admit that, too often, we try to obey, follow, believe and so on, whereas Jesus is looking for a personal, loving relationship.

You could develop the theme with the rest of verse 15 – 'more than these'. These what? These other disciples? These surroundings? These boats and fish? Question whether Jesus has our first love. He deserves it!

> **Quote:** 'There is no wood like the wood of the cross for lighting the fire of love in the soul.' (Elizabeth of the Trinity)

Service: Show how Jesus calls Peter to three specific jobs in verses 15–17. Don't get stuck with what these meant: the point is that Jesus has work for all who meet him. Are we ready to serve the Master?

Suffering: Show how Jesus is straight and honest with Peter in verses 18–19: meeting Jesus is hard; it brings challenges. His friends down the years have found this.

> **Quote:** 'She took the alabaster jar of her life and broke it and gave the ointment of her service to him and his cause.' (W. P. Livingstone, speaking of Mary Slessor, a Scottish missionary to Nigeria in the late nineteenth and early twentieth century)

Starting: Explain how language is sometimes limited, with verses 15–17 needing explanation:

> **Quote:** ' "Do you love me?" "Yes," Peter replied. "You know I am your friend." "Do you *really* love me?" "Yes, Lord," Peter said, "You know I am your friend." "Are you even my friend?" Peter was grieved at the way Jesus asked the question this third time. "Lord, you know my heart; you know I am." (From Living Bible, following J. B. Phillips)

Point out how Jesus comes down to Peter's level. He asks three times, covering the three denials (John 18:17, 25–27) and comes to the only response Peter can give ('friend', c.f. 'love').

> **Quote:** 'What a long way it is between knowing God and loving him!' (Blaise Pascal)

Simplicity: Show how Jesus actually begins again with Peter: he uses his old name (verse 17 – compare Mark 3:16) and recalls the first words ever exchanged (end of verse 19 – compare Mark 1:16). Jesus can begin again with us.

Ending: Run through the 'Ss', inviting your hearers to meet Jesus (or meet him again) this Eastertide.

> **Quote:** 'And yet I want to love thee, Lord.
>   O light the flame within my heart,
>   And I will love thee more and more –
>   Until I see thee as thou art.'
>   (Bishop W. Walsham How, last verse of his
>   hymn 'It is a Thing Most Wonderful')

20. April 25: St Mark

WHEN: St Mark's Day (April 25). Lent. Good Friday. Advent. Second in a mini-series, 'What is the Gospel?'

WHO: Older people.

AIM: This talk is about heaven: how Jesus has brought heaven to us and how we can go to heaven.

HINTS: If the mini-series is being followed, you will have spoken of Jesus as 'God with us' from talk 27. Because God is with us, heaven is now with us, too. We are looking at the start and finish of each Gospel: hence the readings.

This talk can easily be adapted for Lent and Good Friday. With its theme, it could form part of an Advent series, or would be good for older people.

BIBLE READINGS: Mark 1:9–13; 15:33–39.

OUTLINE:
Way in: Have you ever seen anything really dramatic? Talk about it briefly, leading to what you want to share: the two most dramatic events ever seen in the history of the world (which is a pretty dramatic opening in itself!).

Mark gives us two great incidents relating to heaven:

1. **Heaven – has come.** If you can, capture the excitement of the first reading: 'Come with me back in time. We are standing by a river. . .' Make the incident with John the Baptist come alive again. Get your hearers to sense the drama. Ask the questions: How far away would you need to be to see a dove fly? From how far away could you hear a voice speak, without shouting or amplification? If using a microphone, you could demonstrate.

So – how far away was heaven that day? There is a heaven: Jesus brought it very near to us. It is much nearer than the old hymn suggests:

> **Quotes:** 'There's a home for little children
> Above the bright blue sky.'
> (Albert Midlane, from the hymn
> 'There's a Friend for Little Children')

> 'Earth's crammed with heaven
> And every common bush afire with God;
> But only he who sees takes off his shoes.
> The rest sit round it and pluck blackberries.'
> (Elizabeth Barrett Browning, from her poem 'Aurora Leigh')

Why don't we see it? 2 Corinthians 4:4 helps. This world has blinded us from seeing the next. We need Jesus to open our eyes to the truth and reality of heaven: how wonderful that heaven is here!

2. **Heaven – I'm coming.** Do your 'Come with me. . .' once again. Take your hearers to the Temple, showing them the seamless curtain separating us from the Holy of

Holies – no way in to God. Go to the second reading. Get your hearers to watch Jesus die. At the moment of death, get them to run with you back into the city, rushing into the Temple, climaxing with the sensational words of Mark 15:38.

By his death, Jesus has opened the gate of heaven for us to go through. This is the great truth: we can go through the curtain right into the home of God. It's not a fairy story.

Quote: 'The true reality is the one you can't see.' (From a song by Stuart Penny)

We can know heaven with us now. The 'dove' of the Holy Spirit, the voice of the Father, is for us now.

Ending: Heaven has been torn open for Jesus to be here. He has torn open the way back to heaven for us (it's the same word in Mark 1:10 and 15:38).

Quote: 'It ought to be for us a matter of supreme concern to make sure that we shall be among those who enter the narrow door.' (David Gooding, *According to Luke*)

Let's receive heaven and get into it now, living as members even while here on earth!

21. Ascension Day

WHEN: Ascension Day. Sunday before/after.

AIM: Partly to speak of the Ascension, partly to encourage Christians to share their faith with God's help.

BIBLE READINGS: Acts 1:1–11; Matthew 28:16–20.

OUTLINE: 'He ascended into heaven' (the Apostles' Creed). What did Jesus do on this unique day? He did things for the past, present and future.

The past: mission announced: It is worth checking Matthew 28:19–20, Mark 16:15 and Acts 1:8 for different emphases on the same theme. We are to share our faith with others, because that was the last command of Jesus before he ascended to heaven. We are to do this by our lives:

> **Quote:** 'Ministry is what I leave in my tracks as I follow Jesus.' (A friend of Leighton Ford, the Canadian evangelist, in conversation)

This is the work of the whole church: it is not the only work, but, as the last command, is crucial.

> **Quote:** 'We must be fishers of men, and not keepers of the aquarium.' (Dr C. V. Hill)

Point out that the disciples obeyed (Mark 16:20). Do we?

Quote: 'To bring the life of the Nation under the Word of God – that is what the task of the Church is.' (John Gibbs, former Bishop of Coventry, May 1983)

The present: mission assured: Good news: we are not sent out, like the Charge of the Light Brigade, to almost certain failure. There is not even a 'maybe it'll work, off you go'.

Share the assurances of Acts 1:5 and 8. As it then came true for those disciples (Acts 2:4), so it does for us. The promises at the end of Matthew 28:20 and in Mark 16:20 are for today. Jesus assures us of his presence and power.

Quote: 'In the days of his earthly ministry, only those could speak to him who came where he was. If he was in Galilee, men could not find him in Jerusalem; if he was in Jerusalem, men could not find him in Galilee. But his Ascension means that he is perfectly united with God; we are with him wherever we are present to God; and this is everywhere and always.' (Archbishop William Temple)

Past, present . . . and into. . .

The future: mission accomplished: 'All authority in heaven and on earth has been given to me' (Matthew 28:18). Then, 'He was taken up' to heaven (Acts 1:9).

Quote: 'He ascended into heaven and is seated at the right hand of the Father.' (The Nicene Creed)

Reference can be made to Mark 16:19 and the splendid Hebrews 1:3.

Quote: 'Jesus the Saviour reigns
The God of truth and love.
When he had purged our stains
He took his seat above.
Lift up your heart, lift up your voice,
Rejoice; again I say, rejoice.'
(Charles Wesley, hymn)

Jesus has won! He is Lord.

Ending: Our mission is to share in the victory of Jesus. The ascension is the assurance of this: we now have the Holy Spirit in our Christian lives, work and witness. We must enter into this victory and obey the last command to 'go'.

An ending of dedication mingled with praise, thanks and adoration would be appropriate.

22. Pentecost

WHEN: Pentecost.

AIM: To show the vital place of the Holy Spirit and to speak of what he does.

HINT: If you do not preach long sermons, there could be a three-part mini-series here, for Pentecost and the two subsequent Sundays, or for any time outside major festivals. Whether in one or three sermons, we are looking at the authority of the Holy Spirit, so you need to believe in his authority to preach about it.

BIBLE READINGS: Joel 2:25–29; Acts 2:1–4.

OUTLINE: Introduce this talk by saying what a vital subject you are about to share. The Holy Spirit wants to change our lives and our church in three great areas.

The Holy Spirit's authority in redemption: The Holy Spirit is central in creation and re-creation. He was there in the beginning (Genesis 1:2), involved in creation. It was through the Spirit that Jesus was able to go to the cross (Hebrews 9:14).

Having helped Jesus buy our redemption, the Spirit now comes to do his vital work of showing us our need of change, convincing us of our need: John 16:8–11 is key here. Then, as Jesus told Nicodemus, we can only become Christians through the Spirit (John 3:8): we cannot make it without him.

> **Quote:** 'Children of the Resurrection, sons of the Holy Spirit.' (Archbishop Donald Coggan, in his enthronement sermon in Canterbury Cathedral)

That is just the start. Now comes. . .

The Holy Spirit's authority in renewal: This is to make us the Christians God wants us to be. It comes in two parts:

1. **His fruit.** Galatians 5:22–23 are the key verses here. If this is a single sermon, detail the fruit briefly. Ask if these qualities are to be found in your hearers, whatever anyone else may say critically. . .

   > **Quote:** 'Do what the Holy Spirit prompts. Better offend ten thousand friends than grieve the Spirit of God.' (Evan Roberts of Welsh Revival fame)

2. **His gifts.** These are very varied, but for every one of us (1 Corinthians 12:7). You could refer to the leadership gifts of Ephesians 4:11, or to the gifts throughout Romans 12 and 1 Corinthians 12.

   The vital aspects here are that the gifts come very specifically from the Spirit as he wills (1 Corinthians 12:11); and we must not only receive the gifts, but use them for the blessing of each other (1 Peter 4:10).

We need the Holy Spirit to run our lives as Christians. Sadly, both individuals and whole churches often fall a long way short. Which leads to your third area of the Holy Spirit's authority:

The Holy Spirit's authority in revival: It was never God's plan for us to be weak. The Spirit comes to us collectively and personally:

1. The church.

> **Quote:** 'A sober church never does any good. At this hour we need men drunk with the Holy Spirit.' (Leonard Ravenhill, *Why Revival Tarries*)

> Show how (from Acts 2:1–4), when the Spirit came at Pentecost, the church was filled with the Holy Spirit. Say that this applies especially to you, the preacher:

> **Quote:** 'The best way to revive a church is to build a fire in the pulpit!' (D. L. Moody)

2. Each one. After the 'drunk' quote, Ephesians 5:18 is good! You could speak of John the Baptist's promise regarding Jesus – see Matthew 3:11.

> **Quote/Story:** A London committee discussed whether to invite American evangelist, D. L. Moody, to England. One member asked, tetchily, 'Has Mr Moody a monopoly of the Holy Spirit?' 'No', was the reply, 'but the Holy Spirit has a monopoly of Mr Moody.'

Ending: We need the Holy Spirit!

> **Quote:** 'One baptism, many fillings, constant anointing by the Holy Spirit.' (Dr Stephen Olford)

Do you dare to end your talk by asking your hearers to allow the Holy Spirit to fall on you all right now?

23. Pentecost

WHEN: Pentecost.

AIM: To encourage Christians to know the fullness of the Holy Spirit, with all that that means for life.

HINTS: It may be worth flicking through the previous chapters of Ezekiel to get the background for this talk. This is a talk you need to believe experientially: if you've not got it, you may struggle to give it. The verses are all from the reading, unless stated otherwise.

BIBLE READING: Ezekiel 47:1–12.

OUTLINE:
Introduction: Tell your hearers that picture language is brilliant.

> **Quote:** 'One picture is worth ten thousand words.' (Frederick Barnard, *Printer's Ink*, 1927)

Say how today's reading paints an amazing picture for us of God at work in our lives. You could, very briefly, give the background of the Temple having been destroyed and God giving the design for a new building (Ezekiel 40 – 46). The secret of its success is in the reading: it is the secret for our success as Christians.

The need: Say how religion can be very 'dry', as can our Christian lives. We need the water of God's Holy Spirit. God sends his river (verse 1). Draw from the great New Testament references to the Holy Spirit, especially those involving fullness, and those where the Holy Spirit is pictured as springing water.

You could start with John 10:10, going back to John 4:13–14, which shows Jesus as the source. A really key passage is John 7:37–39, another wonderful 'picture', which fits with 1 Corinthians 6:19. Emphasise how we all need this filling of the Holy Spirit – he is not an 'optional extra'.

> **Quote:** 'Many priests need to be evangelised. A good dose of the Holy Spirit would do the Ministers of our land a world of good.' (Father Pat Lynch – Roman Catholic).

Say that our first need is to be filled. Then we can see two results:

Depth: Take your hearers through verses 3–5: 'ankle', 'knee', 'waist' and 'over-the-top' (verse 5, author's paraphrase!). This picture language gives you the perfect way to ask, 'How deep are our Christian lives?' Ask if we are just paddling about ('ankle'), or sort of half-and-half ('knee', 'waist'). Talk of the tragedy of playing at being Christians, of not being filled with the Spirit. We need so much of the Spirit that we are able to offer him to others, too.

> **Quote:** ' "I can't hold much," a sweet old lady told me one day. "But I can overflow lots, you know." ' (Leith Samuel)

Effectiveness: There are so many things you could say, but here are four suggestions:

1. **The river flows east** (verse 3). From Jerusalem, that means towards the Dead Sea (verse 8). Show how this means new life (verses 8–9), leading to the point that we are to bring God's Spirit to others, that they may live, through Jesus.

2. **The river makes the area beautiful** (verse 7). Ask if your hearers are allowing the Holy Spirit to change them for the better.

   Quote: 'As Christians, we are not so much concerned with reputation as character.' (John Boyd, when General Secretary of the AUEW Trade Union)

3. **The river reproduces life** (verse 9). Are we actually winning others for Jesus Christ?

4. **The river produces fruit** (verse 12). Bring in Galatians 5:22–23 – the fruit of the Spirit.

The secret: 'The water from the sanctuary flows to them' (verse 12) is imperative for us.

   Quote/Story: The brother of the great preacher C. H. Spurgeon was asked by a shopkeeper what was the secret of his brother's success. 'I think,' he answered, 'that it lies in the fact that he loves Jesus of Nazareth, and that Jesus of Nazareth loves him.'

Ending: Urge your hearers to 'be filled with the Spirit' (Ephesians 5:18).

24. Trinity Sunday

WHEN: Trinity Sunday. 'Tricky Questions' session.

AIM: To help people start to understand and accept the triune nature of the one God.

HINT: This is a very tough subject. If you could write a brief, understandable book explaining the doctrine of the Trinity, it would sell in its millions! Keep this talk simple, however complex the problem in understanding the Trinity.

VISUAL AID: You will need to prepare an acetate/Power-Point: see later.

BIBLE READINGS: Philippians 2:5–11; Matthew 3:13–17.

OUTLINE:
Introduction: You could use some of the 'hint' above to say how you have a very tricky subject today, yet a vital one for our faith.

> **Quote:** 'Above all else, what distinguishes the God of Christianity from the gods of all other faiths is the conviction of God as Trinity.' (Clive Calver)

Ask your hearers if they believe in a trinitarian deity.

Quotes: 'God in three persons, blessed Trinity.' (Bishop R. Heber, from the hymn 'Holy, Holy, Holy')

'Thrice holy! Father, Spirit, Son.
Mysterious Godhead, Three in One.'
(E. Cooper, from the hymn 'Father of Heaven, Whose Love Profound')

There is one God: Say how vital this is: other religions think we have three Gods. Draw from Exodus 20:1-3, emphasising the 'I'. Ephesians 4:4-6 and 1 Corinthians 8:6 prove your point.

There are three persons in the Godhead:

1. God the Father. Say how we all agree on this one: he is 'the Lord your God' of Exodus 20:2.

2. God the Son. You could start with a verse from the Philippians reading: the word 'Lord' (*kurios*) is used for 'God' (Yahweh) 6,156 times in the Septuagint (Old Testament). Exactly the same word 'Lord' is used in Philippians 2:11. That would bring you to John 1:1, 14 and, especially, 18.

Quote: 'If Shakespeare were to come into this room, we should all rise up to meet him, but if that Person (Jesus) were to come into it, we should all fall down and try to kiss the hem of his garment.' (Charles Lamb)

3. God the Holy Spirit. The key for you here is to show

that the Holy Spirit has all the characteristics of God. He is holy (1 Corinthians 6:19); eternal (Hebrews 9:14); all-powerful (Luke 1:35); omnipresent (Psalm 139:7); the Spirit of God (1 Corinthians 2:10) and can be blasphemed (Matthew 12:31).

You could refer to Acts 5:3–4: 'You have lied to the Holy Spirit . . . to God.'

The three persons are different: This is easily shown from the Matthew reading, which has all three in action, working together.

The problem: how?

Quote: 'When the question is asked, "Three what?" human language labours altogether under great poverty of speech. The answer however is given, "three persons," not that it may be spoken but that it might be left unspoken.' (St Augustine)

Say how, in 1315, Raymond Lull, a pioneering missionary to Muslims, explained the Trinity as a triangle: one triangle, three corners – each necessary for the one triangle:

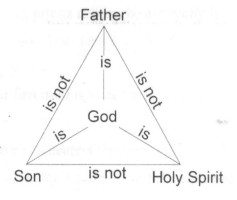

You might point out that Lull was martyred as a result!

Conclusion: Admit that you have not explained the Trinity! But we have a trinitarian creation (Father: Genesis 1:1; Son: John 1:3; Spirit: Genesis 1:2) and a trinitarian re-creation: God the Father sends God the Son who gives us God the Holy Spirit.

Ending: Here is a lovely prayer you could use:

Quote: 'In the mystery of your Godhead you have revealed to us the fullness of your divine glory. We praise you, Father, with the Son and the Spirit, three persons, equal in majesty, undivided in splendour, yet one Lord, one God, ever to be worshipped and adored.' (Prayer for Trinity Sunday, *New Zealand Prayer Book*, 1989)

25. August 6: Feast of the Transfiguration

WHEN: Feast of the Transfiguration. Sunday before/after. 'Tricky Questions' session. Bible Sunday.

AIM: To show the uniqueness of Jesus.

EXPLANATION: This talk gives a different 'angle' on the transfiguration because it uses a different biblical passage to explain a key moment of that incident – the disciples being told to listen exclusively to Jesus. The talk can, therefore, be used to answer the difficult question, 'Why is Jesus unique?' or to help Christians understand the absolute importance of Jesus.

BIBLE READINGS: Acts 4:5–22; Mark 9:2–8.

OUTLINE:
Introduction: It might be good to open with a shock: 'The Bible makes some outrageous claims! They were shocking when they were made and they still are today!' Explain how the transfiguration gave rise to Peter making one such claim. Describe the incident in Mark 9, with God's words in verse 7. Peter heard it and later spoke as he did in Acts 4:12 – your key verse.

Throwing down the gauntlet: Show how Peter came to say this: backtrack briefly through the healing of the lame man (Acts 3:1–10) and the challenge about this in 4:7. You could show how Peter had heard the words at the transfiguration and, subsequently, had witnessed the unique death and resurrection and had been filled with the Holy Spirit's power (Acts 2:4). That was why he spoke as he did to the lame man (3:6). His words in 4:12 were a shock to the religious leaders.

> **Quote:** 'Jesus was able to satisfy their soul's hunger as nothing else had done.' (David Gooding, *In the School of Christ*)

The challenge was the uniqueness of Jesus, you can point out: he himself threw down the gauntlet with his famous, 'I am the way, the truth and the life' (John 14:6). Who else makes this claim?

> **Quote:** 'I am still searching for truth.' (Buddha, at the end of his life)

Picking up the challenge: Gauntlets are for accepting, you should explain, asking how this challenge affects us today. Ask what difference the transfiguration makes, with God telling us to listen, supremely, to Jesus (Mark 9:7).

It is worth enquiring if anything has happened, before or since, to negate God's words, or to contradict Peter's challenge in Acts 4:12. Agree that there are many religions, but. . .

> **Quote:** 'Christianity is a religion of salvation, and there is nothing in the other religions of the world to compare with this message of a God who loved, and came after,

and died for, a world of lost sinners.' (John Stott, *Basic Christianity*)

Say that all religions reach up to God but, in Jesus, God uniquely reaches down to us. Go on to show how all religions seek to show ways towards God, whereas Jesus brings the way from God and, therefore, the way back. Only the cross removes the barrier. You could bring in Romans 5:8 here. That is why:

> **Quote:** 'Our message is Jesus Christ; we dare not give less, and we cannot give more.' (Archbishop William Temple)

There are other aspects of the uniqueness of Jesus you can draw on, if time permits, such as his uniquely certain promise of heaven (John 14:2), his offer of fullness of life (John 10:10) and his baptising with the Holy Spirit (Luke 3:16).

> **Quote:** 'John could put repentant people in water: in a sense, anybody could. Only One who was God could put people in the Holy Spirit, or the Holy Spirit in people.' (David Gooding, *According to Luke*)

Ending: Encourage your hearers not to go around saying, 'We're right, you're wrong.' That is not the point. But Jesus is the only way: use Acts 4:12 one last time.

> **Quote:** 'The only hope for our society is Jesus Christ.' (Bobby Ball, the fall-guy comedian, half of the Cannon and Ball comedy duo)

26. September 1

WHEN: Start of new term. January 1. Advent Sunday. Nearest Sunday to September 1 and January 1. Church anniversary.

AIM: To get churches, groups and organisations kick-started for a new season of activity. Advent Sunday is the traditional beginning of the church's year, but other dates apply, especially a new start after the summer holidays.

HINT: This is a talk to inspire hope and action, to encourage a new beginning. Give it with positive enthusiasm. (Verses from Isaiah 43, unless stated.)

BIBLE READINGS: Isaiah 43:14–21; Ephesians 2:11–22.

OUTLINE:
Introduction: Start by talking of the milestone you have all reached, whatever the occasion (above), saying how it is time to move on. Hopefully. . .

The past was great: Begin on a light-hearted note, with verse 18 saying one thing, but following a great past story in verses 16–17! Agree that it is good to look back at what God has done, especially in making us Christians.

Quote: 'In France, there is a book similar to the English *Doomsday Book*. One entry is for the village of Domrémy. Across the whole page is written "Taxes remitted for the Maid's sake". It was the birthplace of Joan of Arc. In the same way, Jesus has remitted our sins.' (Michael Green, *Choose Freedom*)

Encourage your hearers to be grateful. But. . .

The present is greater: Use parts of verse 14 – 'Your Redeemer. . .' and compare with parts of the Ephesians reading which speak of Jesus bringing peace through his blood (Ephesians 2:14) and that we now have this peace today (2:17) and a new relationship with God (2:18).

Quote: 'In my early Christian experience I was taught that I was to stick to Christ. That was very good; but there is something I have found out since, and that is that Christ sticks to me.' (Henry Moorhouse)

You could go back, in the Isaiah reading, to verse 1 to show this personal relationship with the only Saviour (verse 11). Encourage your hearers to enjoy a current relationship with God.

The future is greatest: This is your major emphasis. You could mention the ultimate future:

Quote: 'His heart grew weak, but he was looking forward to eternal life.' (Fiona Castle, about her husband, Roy, as he was dying of cancer)

But bring your hearers to verses 18–19 to show God's good plans for the future here.

Quote: 'Grow old along with me,
The best is yet to be:
The last of life, for which the first was made.
Our times are in his hand.'
(Robert Browning, from the poem 'Rabbi ben Ezra')

You will need to update the promise of verse 20, showing how the 'jackals' – those who seek to attack us – will be under God's control, and the 'owls' – those who watch – will always keep an eye on us. Use the lovely 'water in the desert' to speak of us bringing new life and hope to a thirsty world. Here is a splendid future for us all.

Quote: 'Christ turns all our sunsets into dawns.'
(Clement of Alexandria)

Use verse 21 to share the joy of worship for our future, too.

Ending: Underline, from the whole reading, God's love for your hearers, individually and collectively. Say how we are to go into the future in the certainty of this, trusting God for whatever comes.

Quote: 'It is not for us to discern the future, it is for us to be faithful.' (George Carey, when Archbishop of Canterbury)

If you want to end on a fun note:

Quote: 'I've got shoes with grown-up laces,
I've got knickers and a pair of braces,
I'm all ready to run some races.
Who's coming out with me?'
(A. A. Milne, 'Growing up', poem from *When We Were Very Young*)

27. September 21: St Matthew

WHEN: Feast of St Matthew. Sunday before/after. Ascension Day. Christmas. Short talk. First in mini-series (see also talks 20, 31 and 38). Bible Sunday.

AIM: To show the great message of Matthew, where his Gospel brings the amazing news of 'God with us'.

HINTS: There are, as the 'When' section shows, several options. The points can be made briefly for a short talk (say at a Christmas school assembly or a carol service) or, emphasising the second section, for Ascension Day. With the mini-series, this gives a launch-pad for the next three.

VISUAL AIDS: A pair of bookends.

BIBLE READINGS: Matthew 1:18–25; 28:16–20.

OUTLINE:
Introduction: If you have a pair of bookends, they could demonstrate what you are going to say: Matthew has an amazing book, with the bookends at either end showing what he's telling us inside.

The front: Tell the story, briefly, of Jesus being born, from

1:18–25. The key is verse 23 (echoing Isaiah 7:14): make a big thing of it.

> **Quote:** 'The potter becomes the clay.' (Alan Boddington)

Talk about how God has not stayed away, letting us desperately seek and not find him. Nor has he let us mess up life without his coming to rescue us. Say how Matthew wants us to know this unique news right at the beginning of his Gospel. You could note how all religions in the world are reaching up to God: now God has returned the compliment (verse 23).

> **Quote:** 'Do you think it a small thing to have the secret of the Lord of lords with you, and to be called the friends of God?' (George Whitefield)

The back: It would be good to ask, 'Lucky world – God around for 33 years – but what now?' Sensational news: Matthew's got another bookend. Read the very last verse (28:20).

> **Quote:** 'In the Old Testament it was God *for* his people. That was wonderful. In the Gospels, it was Immanuel, God *with* his people. But in the Acts of the Apostles and in the Epistles it is best of all, God *in* his people.' (Tom Rees)

Take your hearers to 28:18, showing Jesus to have full authority to make his promises stay true. Hebrews 13:5 underlines what you are saying. God has come to be with us: but he has not left us at the ascension of Jesus. He is always here. Say how thrilling it is that, whatever we are doing, Jesus stays with us.

Quote: 'It is not possible for us to spend all our time with words of prayer on our lips, but it is possible for us to be all our days in a spirit of prayer, realising our dependence on God for all we have and are, being conscious of his presence with us wherever we may be, and yielding ourselves continually to him to do his will.' (Leon Morris)

The middle: You certainly do not have enough time to deal with the other 26 chapters! But a reference to 11:28 would not be out of place, speaking of how, if God is with us, we need to come to be with him. Then we will be sure of a permanent relationship with God, whatever happens.

Quote/Story: The Methodist open-air preacher, Lord Soper, was asked what was the best advice he had ever been given. He replied that his first minister had told him, 'Those who have heard God speak can bear his silence.'

Ending: When the Verdi opera, *Aida*, is performed at the vast amphitheatre in Verona, two huge identical sphinxes are erected on either side of the stage to protect the action. In the same way, you can say how Matthew has erected his two great protectors for his Gospel: 'God with us' and 'I am with you always'. Encourage your hearers to let these protect them, too.

28. Harvest

WHEN: Harvest. School assembly.

WHO: Men. Older People. Children. New Christians.

AIM: To encourage people to know Jesus as the Saviour and protector of their lives.

VISUAL AIDS: An old pair of gardening gloves (with holes at the finger-tips, if possible). A smart pair of gloves. (Both pairs yours.)

HINT: This is a very visual talk: make the most of the actions suggested. Adapt it with your own gardening stories, though the aim is not to exhibit your green-fingered prowess! Vary the talk according to your audience.

BIBLE READINGS: Romans 13:8–14; Colossians 3:1–17.

OUTLINE: The gloves prove your points.

Worthless gloves: You could start in the Garden of Eden (this is a Harvest-style, gardening talk). God made everything great and gave us his protection (put best gloves on). But we chose to do it our way (gloves thrown on floor). The result? Disaster.

Relate a nasty garden story of how you got cut/stung because you weren't wearing the right protection (a scar would help. . .). Gloves are worthless if they are off.

What a mess we've got into – Colossians 3:5–9. We have spoiled our lives before God.

Quote: 'You must know God as an enemy before you know him as a friend.' (Martin Luther)

Waiting gloves: Speak of Jesus coming into our world, always living as we should (put on best gloves). Picture his hands (with gloves on) welcoming, healing, blessing (do the actions). At the cross, they stripped him (Luke 23:34): take off the gloves. He took our place and our sins.

Quote: 'He took our curse, so that we might receive his blessings.' (John Stott, *The Cross of Christ*)

God brought him back (gloves back on): now he offers us new life (gloves taken off, held towards hearers).

Wearing gloves: 'Put on the Lord Jesus Christ' (Romans 13:14).

Quote: 'We are dust, dignified by divinity.' (Jill Briscoe)

Ephesians 4:24 shows how we become new people. If you are using the Colossians reading, verses 12–15 work well here. What a wonderful life: new, free and bringing blessing to you and others.

Working gloves: Say that you are going to tell the whole truth: you have another pair of gloves. Produce the old gardening gloves – hopefully with laughter. Put them on.

Gloves are not only for beauty; they are also for hard work. Talk a little (not too much) about your work in the garden – the digging, the weeding – with no one watching. Explain how being a Christian is often like that.

Quote/Story: In the film *A Man For All Seasons*, Thomas More has a young man working with him called Richard Rich, who wants to be a political leader. 'Become a teacher,' More tells him. 'But who would see me?' 'Your pupils, your friends, God. Not a bad audience,' More replies.

It is good – and very hard – to 'put on the Lord Jesus Christ'.

Quote/Story: When Saint Gregory Nazianzius was baptised in the fourth century, he consecrated to God 'all my goods, my glory, my health, my tongue and my talents'.

Winning gloves: Your old gloves are winners: mention your prize onions, delicious parsnips, amazing tomatoes and so on (enthusiastically and briefly). If you have holes in the finger-tips, show how the gloves protect you as you pick mouth-watering blackberries without getting pricked! We become winners with Jesus: the fruit of the Spirit in Galatians 5:22–23. We gain life itself, now and for ever.

Quote: 'Eternal life is not a life which begins after death. Those who live in Christ have already, in him, risen from the dead.' (Michel Quoist, *Meet Christ and Live*)

Ending: Hold out the good gloves again: 'Put on the Lord Jesus Christ.' John 6:37 is a lovely promise. Be sure to lead a prayer of response.

29. Harvest

WHEN: Harvest. Advent.

WHO: Older people.

AIM: To show how vital it is to be part of God's kingdom while we have both time and opportunity.

HINT: This is a serious talk. Both Harvest and Advent hold special challenges and, sometimes, we need to have the courage to present them. You will need to decide if you have the nerve. Since the theme of this talk is so vital, if you do not ever give it, ask yourself why not.

BIBLE READING: Matthew 13:24–30, 36–46.

OUTLINE:
Introduction: Admit that some things scare you (spiders, flying, muggers or whatever). But there is a verse in the Bible which scares you – Jeremiah 8:20: 'The harvest is past, the summer has ended, and we are not saved.' Say how Harvest sounds fun, but it carries a health warning.

'The harvest is past': Enthuse how wonderful Harvest is – the whole year has been heading here. Explain that the world is heading to harvest, as John the Baptist forecast (Matthew 3:12). Show how Jesus agreed: he speaks 600 verses in Matthew, with over 200 about his second coming, and heaven and hell (as Matthew 13:30).

> **Quote:** 'Men may live as if they owned the world, but they are still only tenants; and the landlord has plans for redevelopment.' (David Gooding, *True to the Faith*)

Rejoice in the good news in John 14:2 and how we can give our thanks.

> **Quote:** 'Come, ye thankful people, come.' (Henry Alford, hymn)

Now confess there is another side: Matthew 13:42, admitting you don't understand it, but you don't like the sound of it. If Jesus warns us, we would be crazy to ignore it, or deny its truth. Ask who knows when this harvest will be. Are we ready?

> **Quote/Story:** Antoine de Saint-Exupéry's book, *Wind, Sand and Stars*, tells of a pilot, lost in the Atlantic: 'Fate has pronounced a decision from which there is no appeal.'

'The summer is ended': Speak of summertime being great and how Jesus is the 'Sun of Righteousness' (Malachi 4:2). Talk of the sunshine of God's love, giving Jesus – after his rescuing death – new life from his resurrection. It is worth everything to get into this sunshine: the stories in Matthew 13:44–46 may help here. Conversely. . .

> **Quote/Story:** The Emperor Charlemagne had carved on his tomb, 'What shall it profit a man if he gains the whole world but forfeits his soul?' (Matthew 16:26)

Summer will end. You could use God's warning in Genesis 6:3a. We need to come into God's sunshine, to come home to him.

Quote/Story: The writer G. K. Chesterton was absent-minded. He once sent a telegram to his wife, 'Am in Market Harborough. Where should I be?' She replied, 'Home.'

'And we are not saved': Ask if this is true for your hearers: have they been saved by the death of Jesus on the cross? Is his resurrection life in their hearts? Speak of God's love in wanting to make this true.

Quote: 'Millions are spent on medicine to keep our bodies from perishing; on locks to keep our valuables from perishing; but God gave Jesus Christ to keep you from perishing!' (Dr Walter Wilson)

Ending: You could repeat the Jeremiah verse in full, saying how we need to give ourselves unreservedly to Jesus Christ, because he loves us and waits to welcome us as his harvest.

Quote: 'Accept the gifts we offer
For all thy love imparts,
And, what thou most desirest,
Our humble, thankful hearts.'
(Matthias Claudius, translated by Jane Montgomery Campbell, from the hymn 'We Plough the Fields and Scatter')

30. Harvest

WHEN: Harvest. Motivating faith-sharing.

AIM: To take a different approach to Harvest by showing that, as we distribute good things materially, we should share our spiritual produce of blessings with those who are starving in their hearts and souls.

INTRODUCTION: You will need to set the scene, which is why the Bible reading comes after this. Read through 2 Kings 5 and 6. Now tell the story so far: King Ben-Hadad of Aram (Syria) has besieged King Joram and the people of Israel in the city of Samaria. They are dying of hunger as the huge army tightens its grip. But God promises victory via Elisha. Now read on.

BIBLE READING: 2 Kings 7:3–11 (or to verse 16).

OUTLINE: As part two of the introduction, pose the question about what we are giving away at Harvest (not necessary if it is not Harvest). Are we only giving material things, or are we giving the best thing in the world: the good news of eternal spiritual food and drink? It begs answers to three questions:

1. **Have we found good news?** The lepers had (verse 8).

The Western world has in its possessions and provisions. But what about our spiritual wealth?

If you are brave, you can have an 'audience participation time'. Ask them to answer out loud to the following questions: 'Do you believe God is real?' 'Do you believe he loves us?' 'Did he send Jesus to be our Saviour?' 'Is the resurrection true?' 'Has the Holy Spirit come?' See if you can get a 'Yes' to each one! Then say how most people today don't know these to be true, and how vital they are.

Quote: 'Christianity is a statement which, if false, is of no importance and, if true, is of infinite importance. The one thing it cannot be is moderately important.' (C. S. Lewis)

2. **Have we forgotten good news?** In this delightful incident, the lepers gorged themselves on the food and drink, taking the bounty (verse 8). Alas, the Western world does this materially. Do we take the good things God gives us spiritually and hoard them? Do we selfishly enjoy our worship, fellowship and care for each other? Have we forgotten the Great Commission of Matthew 28:19–20? Yes, our internal practices are important – but the sharing with others is vital.

Or have we forgotten God's power to reach the lost?

Story: A small boy goes to an Anglican 1662 Matins. He is pleased with the Lord's Prayer, as he knows it, saying it enthusiastically. When it is prayed the second time, he prays it even louder, but is embarrassed when the congregation stops at 'deliver us from evil', while he continues in the silence! At home, his father tries to help him. 'Why do you think they didn't carry on?' he asks. The boy replies, 'Perhaps they forgot about the power and the glory.' (Told by David Prior in *The Suffering and the Glory*)

The challenge is brilliantly put in Esther 4:14. Do we remain silent?

3. **Will we give good news?** Verses 9 and 10a are excellent, echoed by John and Peter in Acts 4:20.

Quote: 'Good news is news you can shout across the street: "The war is over; the baby's born; God loves you; Christ is risen." ' (Ven. Lorys Davies, when Archdeacon of Bolton)

When we give the good news, we share the work of Jesus: Luke 4:18. You could use the splendid words of Isaiah 62:1. What blessings we have to give this Harvest time!

Quote/Story: Robert Murray McCheyne was the first minister of St Peter's Church, Dundee, from the age of 22 to his death at 29 on March 25, 1843. On his monument outside the church it says, 'He ceased not day and night to labour and watch for souls: and was honoured by his Lord to draw many wanderers out of darkness, into the path of life.'

Ending: Harvest is about giving. If we help materially, why not spiritually? Let's do it!

31. October 18: St Luke

WHEN: St Luke's Day. Sunday before/after. Pentecost. Third in mini-series 'What is the Gospel?'

AIM: To take a different slant on St Luke, whose festival is invariably about healing (see Subject Index for talks on that subject). This talk shows what his Gospel is all about. If part of the mini-series, Luke leads naturally on from Mark (chapter 20) to show the results of heaven coming.

BIBLE READING: Luke 24:36–49.

OUTLINE: Introduce this by talking of the two words which encapsulate everything the world wants – power and peace. The problem is, you can't have the one with the other. Power usually includes strife to get it; peace often means submission. How can we have the two together?

Dr Luke is going to give us the answer! Because of Jesus, we can have both. So. . .

Power brings peace: Try and paint the scene of a world in a mess, far from God. This year? Yes – and 2,000 years ago. Say how God has been planning a rescue and sends his messenger-angel Gabriel: Luke 1:26–27. The key verse is Luke 1:35, emphasising the word 'power'. It is through the greatest power that Jesus comes.

But what sort of power is this? Give a couple of examples of world power today, showing the pain and problems associated with these. Contrast these with the remarkable words of Zechariah as he sings about Jesus in Luke 1:78–79. Where does Jesus 'guide our feet'? Move into the birth of Jesus, with the powerful song of the angels, and its 'Glory to God' which brings 'peace' (Luke 2:14).

Quote: 'The heart-peace of God. . .' (John Worsley)

If you have time to develop this theme, pick out from the following your favourite bits of Luke to show that the power of Jesus brings peace. Otherwise, go to the next heading. Here is a selection of Luke's demonstrations of the power and peace of Jesus:

– The power of the Spirit on Jesus – to do wonderful, positive things (4:18–19).

Quote/Story: Archbishop of the Indian Ocean, Trevor Huddleston, said that the best advice he had ever been given was from an old African woman in Soweto: 'God always minds his own business.'

– 'The power of the Lord' was with Jesus. Why? 'To heal the sick' (5:17).
– By God's power, Jesus raised the dead (7:11–14).
– By his power he calmed the storm (8:24).

Quotes: 'In his will is our peace.' (Dante, *The Divine Comedy: Paradise*)

'All men who live with any degree of serenity live by some assurance of grace.' (Reinhold Niebuhr)

– At least include this one: the loud, powerful voice of Jesus, which buys our peace as he dies (23:46).

Now turn this power and peace around, because. . .

Peace brings power: In chapter 1, Luke had power bringing peace. In the last chapter, Jesus appears after the resurrection. His first word is 'Peace' (24:36). Say how Jesus longs to give this to us. Now move to 24:49 – look what this peace brings. It is 'power' for our lives. Luke's next book will prove this: Acts 2:4.

> **Quote:** 'I'd rather have power with God any time.' (R. T. Kendall)

Ending: Have your hearers got this power and this peace? Encourage them to receive from Jesus and live accordingly.

32. Festival of Lights: October 31

WHEN: Hallowe'en (making it a 'festival of lights'). Christingle (using the candle in the orange). Candlemas. Family service. New Year. Short talk. School assembly.

AIM: To show how Jesus brings light to our lives – and so should we to others.

VISUALS: Two candles (one large, possibly gold, one small). Box of matches. Tray (to catch the wax). Table. Papers.

CAUTIONARY NOTES: Don't get wax on a beautiful table: take a tray/cover. Test your candles first and have plenty of matches.

POSSIBLE HEADINGS FOR THIS TALK:

1. It's not Jesus!
2. It's not me!

BIBLE READING: Matthew 5:13–16. Refer to John 8:12.

OUTLINE: Begin by talking of your untidiness – at home, at work, in the vestry, in your study. Say how you need to get your paperwork under control: you could have a table in front of you scattered with papers and magazines. Your solution has been to get a paperweight. (Produce the large candle, great for sitting on a mess.)

Speak of how the world is also in a mess and needs to be got under control. Give examples (crime, greed, pollution). Christianity has come to bring control – like a big paperweight.

Now is the moment to ask if what you are holding really is a paperweight. Out with the matches, light the candle. Jesus has not come to impose control; he is 'the light of the world' (John 8:12).

Quote: 'I believe in Christianity as I believe that the sun has risen, not only because I see it, but because by it I see everything else.' (C. S. Lewis)

Develop this if there is time. Jesus shines as a light in the darkness: of the 'scary' Hallowe'en, of winter (Christingle), of uncertainty to show the way (New Year).

Quote: 'Darkness is my point of view; light is God's point of view.' (Oswald Chambers)

Burn the match with the candle's flame to show how Jesus burns away our sin by his death on the cross. Blow out the candle to show his death, lighting it again (make sure you have lots of matches!) to demonstrate the resurrection.

With the big candle lit, introduce the small candle. Explain how our church and each one of us can seem like bossy controllers – another paperweight – telling people what to do and (more often) what not to do. Is this how Christianity is perceived by our neighbourhood, friends and families? The Bible reading had Jesus saying to his disciples, 'You are the light of the world' (Matthew 5:14). Now light the little candle from the big candle: we can be the light when Jesus lights up our lives.

Quote: 'Those who have received the Good News can and must communicate and spread it.' (Pope Paul VI, *Evangelii Nuntiandi*)

Ending: There is nothing wrong with paperweights, but candles are much better! We need God's control, but we need the light of Jesus more. If there are non-Christians present you could end with an invitation to let the light of Jesus burn away our sin and light our lives. (I would blow out the little candle before holding the big candle to it once again.)

Quote: 'Thou art my light; if hid, how blind am I!' (Francis Quarles, *Emblems*, 1643)

Alternatively, there could be a prayer, asking God to be our light, helping us to bring that light to others. The evening prayer 'Lighten our darkness' would work.

33. November 11

WHEN: Remembrance Day, or its nearest Sunday. Memorial service. Bereavement. Short talks (a possible mini-series of five). Healing service.

WHO: Older people.

AIM: To show how God wants to rescue us from whatever needy situations we get ourselves into.

HINT: The reading is very long. You could read just one part of it (verses 23–32 would work best) and refer to the rest. As with any talk which tries to make several points, you need to move speedily from one to the next. Alternatively, do each section in turn over five Sundays, using the above verses on Remembrance Sunday. That could get you from Harvest to Advent!

BIBLE READING: Psalm 107.

OUTLINE:
Introduction: If you preach very short sermons, this would make one on its own, giving you six in all! Talk of the needs so many of us have: physical, mental, social and spiritual. Hooray for the opening of Psalm 107: 'The LORD . . . is good.'

Why don't we know this? It is because too many of us do not obey the beginning of verse 2.

Quote: 'When the heart is afire, some sparks will fly out of the mouth.' (Anon)

Say that we Christians should be telling out the news of God's goodness E, W, N & S (verse 3): turn them round: NEWS.

The problems of Psalm 107 are all 'S':

Straying: Talk about how we get lost on life's journey from verses 4–5. Why are we here? Where are we going? (The age-old questions.) Life sometimes seems pointless. On Remembrance Day: Where are all the current wars getting us? We need God's direction.

Quote/Story: Duncan Campbell, at the centre of the 1949 Hebridean revival, heard a young man pray: 'Lord, you have said that you would pour water on the thirsty. Lord, you know I am thirsty for a manifestation of the Man at your right hand. And, Lord, before I sit down, I want you to know that your honour is at stake.'

The lovely words of hope in verses 6–7 echo John 14:6, leading to our thanks (verse 8) and God's full blessings (verse 9).

Sinful: Say how we have a deeper problem, shown in verses 10–16. We get it wrong, as everyone always has.

Quote: 'Adam was only a gardener, and he lost his job through stealing fruit.' (C.H. Spurgeon)

These verses are a picture of the suffering in war and in our personal lives. You could draw on verses 33–34 as well: the physical results of 'man's inhumanity to man' through war and greed, with God seeming far away.

Now bring in God's rescue in verses 13–14 and 35–38. You could use Romans 5:1 to show what Jesus has done as his rescue act from sin.

Sick (verses 17–22): War brings physical and mental suffering through our foolishness (verse 17). In our own lives we suffer, often because of our own folly. But verses 19–20 are great.

> **Quote:** 'Ransomed, healed, restored, forgiven'. (H. F. Lyte, from the hymn 'Praise My Soul')

Show from verses 20–22 how God does want to heal us, so we can rejoice.

Separate (verses 23–32): These verses are often used on Remembrance Day and could be taken in isolation for that day. Paint the graphic picture from verses 23–27. A passing reference to Jonah 1 may be helpful, particularly to show how we get separated from God.

You could say how we are buffeted by life's waves. Then bring your hearers to verses 28–30.

> **Quote:** 'God (but only God!) can actually transform evil into good, so that in retrospect (but only in retrospect!) it is seen to have actually been good, without diminishing in the least the awful actuality of the evil it was at the time.' (Francis Andersen)

Sad: Say how life sometimes just gets us down (verse 39).

Encourage your hearers to discover the resurrection life of
Jesus, with the Holy Spirit renewing them: verses 40–42.

Ending: Whatever the problem, God has shown the
answer each time. Will we heed verse 43?

Quote: 'Christianity is the land of beginning again.'
(W. A. Criswell)

34. Sunday Before Advent: Feast of Christ the King

WHEN: Sunday before Advent (the Feast of Christ the King). Palm Sunday.

AIM: To speak of the greatness of Jesus, and what he wants to do in our lives.

HINT: This is one of those talks where you should be able to speak with wonder and enthusiasm about how ultimately special Jesus is, so go for it! (All verses shown below are from Isaiah 61.)

> **Quote:** 'I cannot say much of great services; yet, if ever my heart was lifted up, it was in preaching of Jesus Christ.' (The Scottish Covenanter, John Livingstone – d. 1672 – on his death bed, quoted by Alexander Smellie, *Men of the Covenant*)

BIBLE READINGS: Isaiah 61; Luke 4:16–21.

OUTLINE:
Introduction: Admit that you are going to indulge yourself today: you are going to speak of your hero, Jesus.

The work of Jesus: Your base is Isaiah 61, which is about Jesus, because he said so (Luke 4:21). Show how Jesus did what he did because of his relationship with the Father and Holy Spirit (verse 1). Jesus comes to do lots of Ss:

Speak: Show how lovely was the message of Jesus (verses 1 and 2): he tells us God's message of salvation. John 1:18 is good.

> **Quote:** 'Jesus put flesh on the bones of God's promise.' (Grace Robinson)

Support: Use the parts of verses 1 and 2 which show the care of Jesus ('to heal. . .', 'to comfort. . .') to help your hearers to see that they can trust a loving Saviour. Ask if they are taking their sorrows and burdens to Jesus.

> **Quote:** 'Kate went to be with her Lord this morning and we know she was ready to be with him. It makes all the difference in the world to know that she is with Jesus, and that he loves her even more than we do. We do not feel any sense of despair.' (Eddie Curry, on the death of his wife, July 2006)

Save: Still in verses 1 and 2, this is where you use 'to proclaim freedom . . . release from darkness. . .'. Talk about us all needing to be set free from our sin by Jesus' death.

> **Quote:** 'The world is a better place because Jesus didn't say, "I don't do crosses." ' (Brandt Gustavson)

Sentence: Point out that Jesus stopped, in Luke 4, halfway through verse 2. But there will be judgement, as that verse shows. Are your hearers trusting Jesus, so that all will be well when judgement comes?

Quote: 'Having a father who ignores wrongdoing sounds great – until you realise that your brother is then free to treat you in any way he wants. Justice demands that if you expect others to face judgement for their actions against you, then you must face the same judgement.' (Peter Meadows)

Sustain: Verse 3 can be spoken of with delight: with salvation comes continuing help and new life.

Seal: Verse 8 can be used to speak of the eternal blessings which seal us for ever.

Our response: Make sure you leave at least a little time to encourage your hearers to do something about all these Ss. Show how we must. . .

– **Receive.** You could show how, when Jesus preached from these words, his message was rejected (Luke 4:20–28). By contrast, we can let verse 10 be true for us.
– **Grow.** Use the second half of verse 3 to show our need to grow up with Jesus.

   Quote. 'Behold the turtle; he makes progress only when he sticks his neck out.' (James Conaut)

– **Glorify.** 'For the display of his splendour' (verse 3, end). Ask if we bring glory to Jesus.
– **Serve.** Verse 6: link with Revelation 1:6.

Ending: This last point would be good for closing: we continue our prayers of worship with going out with this great news.

Quote: 'The saint is neither too busy praying to work, nor too busy working to pray.' (Alan Longworth)

35. Advent

WHEN: Advent Sunday. Any Sunday in Advent. Bible Sunday.

AIM: To convey the excitement of Christ's return and to speak of the urgency of being ready, together with the responsibility of sharing this with others.

HINT: Preach this to yourself first. If you find there are parts you don't believe, ask yourself why not. Of course, you don't have to believe Jesus will return: he will, whether you believe it or not! Although there is a reading, the key verse is Revelation 22:17. In the reading, only the brave go to the end of the paragraph at verse 8.

BIBLE READING: Revelation 20:11 – 21:8.

OUTLINE:
Introduction: You could begin by saying how important certain themes are in the Bible: new birth, mentioned nine times in the New Testament; baptism – 22; repentance – 70 times. We often hear about them. But what about the second coming of Jesus? It is in the New Testament 319 times. For every occasion Jesus' first coming is mentioned, the second coming is mentioned eight times, so this talk is a good theme for Bible Sunday.

Here are three pointers for your Advent talk:

'The day of the Lord will come' (2 Peter 3:10): With not too long to Christmas, say how you are getting ready. If we prepare for this remembrance of the first coming of Jesus, ask what we are doing about his next coming. It may not happen on December 25, but the signs are there to see:

– People laugh at the idea (2 Peter 3:3).
– People love pleasure rather than God (2 Timothy 3:4).
– 'Religion' lacks power (2 Timothy 3:5).
– 'Wars', with 'nation against nation' (Matthew 24:6–7).
– 'Famines and earthquakes' (Matthew 24:7).

You could talk about the state of the world: why doesn't God stop it all? The amazing answer is in 2 Peter 3:9. But – Jesus is coming: 2 Peter 3:10, 1 Thessalonians 5:2.

What will happen when Jesus comes? Show how the reading demonstrates a great division, between Revelation 20:15 and 21:3.

Handle this with care: do not negate the negative: no one spoke about hell more than Jesus himself. He died to save us from it. Like Jesus and the Bible, don't threaten, but warn. However, do speak of the great alternative: we can go to heaven (Revelation 21:2–5).

Quote/Story: Billy Graham tells of a meeting he had with some American senators. The discussion was about optimism and pessimism. Graham was asked what he felt. 'I'm an optimist!' When pressed, he explained, 'I've read the last page of the Bible!' (Billy Graham, *Angels: God's Secret Agents*)

You will need to decide how much time you have to expand this theme. There are some dramatic words in 1 Thessalonians 4:13–18 and 2 Peter 3:10, as well as the reading.

What should we do? This is where you use the key verse: Revelation 22:17 – from the 'last page'. Speak from the three 'comes'.

1. God says 'come': 'the Spirit'. God really wants us to be ready (2 Peter 3:9). That's why Jesus came the first time (Matthew 1:21; Luke 19:10). We must hear and respond to God's call.
2. The church ('the bride') says 'come': that is all of us ('him who hears'). Pose the question, 'Do we?'

   Illustration: As trains reach about 80 mph, speeding out of Euston Station, London, towards the Midlands, travellers see, on their right, the side of a church which proclaims on the whole of its back wall, 'Prepare to meet your God' (from Amos 4:12).

3. We must come (see the rest of the verse).

   Quote: 'When the old Romans used to attack a city, it was sometimes their custom to set up at the gate a white flag and, if the garrison surrendered while the white flag was there, their lives were spared. After that, the black flag was put up and then every man was put to the sword. The white flag is up today.' (C. H. Spurgeon, *Revival Year Sermons*, 1859)

Ending: Urge your hearers to receive the new life of Jesus now, so they are ready. It is the most vital thing they will do: who knows when he will return?

Quote/Story: A little girl heard a clock strike thirteen times. She rushed to her mother, saying, 'It's later than it's ever been before!' (Billy Graham, *Angels: God's Secret Agents*)

36. Christmas

WHEN: Christmas: before, during, after. Family service. Open air at Christmas time.

WHO: Parents.

AIM: To show that the most vital part of Christmas – and life – is a personal relationship with God through Jesus.

HINT: This is a very 'carol-based' talk. The reading (verse 23) has the key words, but you need to get into the service as many of the carols as possible in what follows. You could use the points in the talk to link the carols, making the whole service the talk, without anybody realising!

BIBLE READING: Matthew 1:18–25.

OUTLINE:
Introduction: Can you get a little group to sing the following, to the tune of 'Jingle Bells' (as from 'Dashing through the snow...')?

'Christmas eve is here. As we go off to bed,
As we climb the stairs, nodding sleepy head;
Take our stockings off, hang them in a row,
Then jump quickly into bed and off to sleep we go.

Jingle bells, jingle bells. . .'
(Anon)

Explain that this is a song for parents (fathers, if possible) to
sing with their children as they put them to bed on Christmas Eve.

Talk about how all sorts of things happen at Christmas:
but one amazing fact is often forgotten. So you have a few
quotes to underline part of the reading.

> **Quotes:** 'O come to us, abide with us,
> Our Lord, Immanuel.'
> (From the carol 'O Little Town of Bethlehem',
> Phillips Brooks)
>
> 'O come, O come, Immanuel. . .'
> (First line of the Advent carol from the
> Antiphons in the twelfth-century Latin
> Breviary, translated by J. M. Neale)
>
> 'Pleased as man with man to dwell,
> Jesus, our Immanuel. . .'
> (From the carol 'Hark the Herald Angels Sing',
> by Charles Wesley, as amended by George
> Whitefield)

Now draw on Matthew 1:23 to explain how God seemed
far away, but with Jesus' birth he is now 'with us':
'Immanuel'.

God with us: Talk about your own Christmas. The presents, the puddings, the parties, the paper chains: all great –
but the people make it. Hence the song at the beginning.
The greatest joy is walking upstairs together on Christmas

Eve, singing that song, sitting down to Christmas lunch, watching the telly together. Ask your hearers to remember their best Christmases: it was the togetherness which was best.

Now explain that, for us, the most wonderful thing is having God around to share our lives – at Christmas and always. This makes all the difference.

Quote: 'Xmas and Christmas must never be confused. Christmas is a Christian festival that lasts between Christmas Eve and Epiphany. Xmas is the hysterical six-week anticipation of a brief secular feast that simply cannot stand the weight of anticipation. It is the perfect recipe for anti-climax, if not far worse.' (Simon Barnes, chief sports writer for *The Times*, February 1993)

Us with God: Say how relationships work both ways: we are glad to have our families and they are glad to have us, too. Jesus was glad to have Mary as his mother; we also want God around – and he wants us.

Quote: 'But his mother only, in her maiden bliss,
Worshipped the Beloved with a kiss.'
(From the carol 'In the Bleak Midwinter', by Christina Rossetti)

Now – at this service – God wants us:

Quote: 'What can I give him?. . .What I can . . .
Give him my heart.'
('In the Bleak Midwinter', above)

Ending: Show how God comes to us when we invite him:

Quote: 'O come to us, abide with us,
              Our Lord Immanuel.'
              (As above)

Happy Christmases are together times: you and your heavenly Father.

37. Christmas

WHEN: Christmas. Before/after Christmas. Short talk.

AIM: To show how important it is to receive God's gift of Jesus at Christmas.

HINT: This talk, based on the famous opening verses of St John's Gospel, could be used at a carol service when something brief is needed. But it can easily be longer.

BIBLE READING: John 1:1–14.

OUTLINE:
Introduction: A good start would be to ask your hearers: 'Are you a "Yes, please!" or a "No, thank-you!" type of person?' Explain that God has a gift for us at Christmas: what will we say when it is offered to us?

No, thanks: Talk first about God sending his only Son, Jesus, with all that that would mean – bringing God to us, showing us what God is like, giving his life to pay for our sins, rising to offer new life. Now come to verse 11, speaking of its sadness: even coming to his own people and not being welcomed. Show how we can be just like that.

   Quote: 'For a small reward a man will hurry away on a

long journey, while for eternal life many will hardly take a single step.' (Thomas à Kempis, *The Imitation of Christ*)

You could give a particular challenge to those who come to church, whether regulars or the 'Christmas occasionals', showing how church is often called 'God's house' – 'that which is his own' (verse 11) – in some translations 'his own home'. Do we in his house not really receive him? Ask if we have been coming to this sort of service for many years and yet have not received Christ ourselves.

> **Quote:** 'If you say "No" often enough, God will take you at your word.' (H. L. Ellison)

Yes, please!

> **Quote:** 'Christianity does not mean arguing about Jesus: it means meeting Jesus.' (William Barclay)

Take your hearers to the magnificent words of verse 12, with all their glorious promise, explaining that 'believe' means a step of trust.

> **Quote:** 'In its Greek root, "belief" means simply "to give one's heart to".' (Kathleen Norris, quoted by Philip Yancey in *Reaching the Invisible God*)

Speak again of God's gift, this time from the standpoint of Jesus, with his sacrificial leaving of heaven, birth in the poverty of a stable, becoming a refugee, up-bringing in obscurity, suffering and dying that we might be forgiven. If you have a Communion service in your church on Christmas Eve/Day, then say that we do something unique:

Quote: 'On his birthday we celebrate his death day.' (David Bubbers)

Go on to say how hard it was for Jesus to bring the gift (in his death on the cross): it is not so hard for us to receive it.

You could make the point that, if we receive Jesus, we then have a gift for others.

Quote: 'A businessman came to our meeting, went home and called his wife into his study on Christmas morning, put his arm around her and said, "I want to make you the best Christmas present I have ever given you. I want to give you a Christian husband." ' (J. Wilbur Chapman)

Ending: Ask again who is a 'No, thanks' and who is a 'Yes, please!'. A time for silent response would be good.

38. December 27: Feast of St John the Evangelist

WHEN: Feast of St John the Evangelist. Nine lessons and carols. Christmas. Last of mini-series on Gospels.

AIM: This can be a talk for anytime over the Christmas period, but it is also a talk for encouraging a real belief in Jesus and his message.

HINT: Like the other three talks in this mini-series, it is based on both the beginning and the ending of the Gospel – this time John's – but the first half of the talk would make it ideal for a shorter Christmas talk.

BIBLE READING: John 1:1–12.

Introduction:

Quote: 'Paris is very beautiful, but I find no spirituality. Westerners may have wealth and civil liberties, but they are lacking in deeper things. You don't seem to believe in anything.' (Lech Walesa, shortly before becoming President of Poland; it could have been about any British city)

John is a one-track writer. It's as if he has read the other three Gospels and now says to his readers, 'You'd better believe it!' He has two 'bookends': 1:12 and 20:31. At Christmas, you could begin with the Walesa quote and ask if we really believe the message of Christmas, quoting the 1:12 verse.

If this is the final of your mini-series, quote 20:31 as well, asking if we have got to that point. What are we to believe?

Believe the Master: You could say how these first few verses of John are among the greatest pieces of writing ever. But their majesty and beauty should not conceal the dynamite they contain: John wants us to believe their truth.

> **Quote:** 'Most people believe that Jesus is Saviour but not that God is God.' (Michael Baughen, former Bishop of Chester)

Most people also believe that what God wants is for us to do our best and to work for him. It is John who blasts this theory in chapter 6:28–29 – absolutely explosive, then and now. He is even stronger at chapter 3:36. Very pushy! But the truth.

If you have time, you can give instances of how the words and works of Jesus throughout John's Gospel produced belief. Here are a couple:

- The talks Jesus had with the woman at the well and her neighbours led to their believing (4:42).
- In that same chapter, when Jesus healed the son of the royal official, 'he and all his household believed' (4:53).

We are to believe in Jesus. And, secondly . . .

Believe the message: This is where 20:31 comes in. The gospel is not just a 'good story': it is meant to be a life-changing message. We believe the message so we can know the truth.

Quotes: 'I know in order to believe' (Aristotle, the philosopher) is capped by 'I believe in order to understand' (Anselm, the Christian leader).

It is not coincidental that 20:31 follows on immediately after Thomas's great confession of faith (20:28), which is endorsed and extended to us (20:29), encouraging our belief without our seeing.

However, do tell your hearers that John tags on a 'P.S.' to his Gospel: chapter 21 shows that our believing leads to action as we do as Jesus told Peter in 21:19.

Quote: 'Believing and obeying are not two separate moves. When Jesus says to Simon Peter, "Follow me", the response is a simple act of faith and obedience; there is no gap between a mental act of believing and a bodily action of following.' (Lesslie Newbigin, *Proper Confidence*)

Ending:

Quote: 'Only believe, and thou shalt see
That Christ is all in all to thee.'
(John S. B. Monsell, from the hymn 'Fight the Good Fight')

But this is a better ending for Christmas:

Quote: 'Where meek souls will receive him, still
The dear Christ enters in.'
(Phillips Brooks, from the carol 'O Little Town of Bethlehem')

THEMES

39. Bible Sunday: The Bible

WHEN: Bible Sunday. 'Tricky Questions' session (when you can call the talk 'The Problems of the Bible').

WHO: New Christians.

AIM: To face up honestly to the problems the Bible presents and the difficulties of being a Christian.

BIBLE READING: Mark 4:1–20 (verses below from here unless specifically shown to be elsewhere).

OUTLINE:
Introduction: Tell your hearers how hard it is speaking to them! The Bible is a tough book to speak from and a hard book to understand. And what it asks is hard, too. Here is a very honest talk. . .
    You have three problems:

1. **The problem of wisdom.** Who really understands what God is saying in his word? We are in good company (verse 13) – 2 Peter 3:16 is a great comment by Peter about Paul!
    The secret is to ask Jesus in private, as the disciples did (verse 10). Why does the church wash its dirty linen in

public and talk openly about its difficulties instead of talking them through with each other and Jesus?

Quote: 'Christians claim that Jesus Christ is the Saviour of sinners, but they show no more signs of being saved than anyone else.' (Mahatma Gandhi)

Here are some key verses to give you a real positive: Proverbs 3:7 (we usually quote the previous two verses), 1 Corinthians 2:14 and the splendid answer on how to deal with the problem of wisdom, James 1:5.

2. **The problem of work.** Once we get the Bible and begin to understand it, we have then to go out with its message: verses 3 and 14. The Bible, God's word, is for sharing. Most of the story of the sower is of hard, unrewarding work.

It would be good to give one or two examples from other areas of life where people work very hard, often without anyone else seeing. Politics is one area, where people work very hard to get votes for their candidates.

Quote: 'We have all got to work, and we have got to work until we drop. And then we have got to pick ourselves up and go on working.' (Chris Patten, Conservative Party Chairman, before the 1992 General Election)

If they can do it for that, why can't we in sharing God's wonderful, eternal word with others? Another example could be to contrast a lifeboat 'open day', when everyone applauds, with the unseen and dangerous rescues in the middle of the night by volunteers, who then come ashore to go to their regular daytime jobs.

Is it hard to share God's word? Yes, often. But. . .

Quote: 'We must be warriors, not worriers.' (George Green)

3. **The problem of winning.** We want success. But the sower seems a failure. (Three-quarters doesn't succeed and only one-third of the seed on good soil produces 100 per cent.)

We are called to believe the Bible, work with it and be faithful.

Quote: 'I would rather attempt something great for God and fail than attempt nothing for God and succeed.' (Robert Schuller)

The question in Luke 18:8 is a hot one. Will we be faithful to God's word?

Ending: Say how amazing it is for God to have written to us and spoken to us as he has. The challenge is to love the Bible, share its message and be faithful to the God who gave it to us.

40. Church

WHEN: Mothering Sunday. Any Sunday when you want to talk about church.

AIM: To explain what church is all about and to encourage every member to play their part, while recognising the value of every other member.

CONFESSION: We talk of 'Father God'. As the church is 'the bride' of Christ (Revelation 21:9), people speak of 'Mother Church'. Forgive, therefore, the fact that the headings spell MUM. . . .

BIBLE READING: Ephesians 4:7–16.

OUTLINE:

Introduction: Start out by asking what we are doing here in church today. You could suggest things like praising, praying, proclaiming. Yes – but what does it mean to be 'church'?

M for ministry: Say how two things are vital to make church work.

1. **Leadership.** Quote verse 11 from the reading, explaining the variety of 'up-front' gifts. You will have to decide

if you believe that all these gifts still exist today (there is no evidence that they do not). Comment briefly on each one, for example. . .

Quote: 'Evangelists are the rank-and-file missionaries of the church.' (William Barclay)

Now ask: Who are these people in our church? Or do we expect the minister to be all of them? Do we push one person too far?

Joke: A mother knocks on her son's bedroom door. 'Go to church!' A sleepy voice replies, 'Why should I?' 'Go to church!' 'Give me three good reasons!' 'Number 1, I'm your mother and I'm telling you to. Number 2, you're 41 years old and old enough to go by yourself. Number 3, you're the minister!' (Gert Doonenbal)

The whole point of leadership is in verse 12: speak of how important this is – we are all meant to be moving forward to play our part.

2. **Ownership.** Ask who agrees with verse 7. Using the end of verse 8, ask, 'What did you get?'

Quotes: 'Paul does not envisage that any member of the church will be a mere spectator to its worship and involvement with mission.' (William Lane, commenting on verse 8, from *Scripture Union Bible Study Books – Ephesians to 2 Thessalonians*)

'Church life has been turned into a comfortable ghetto, instead of being an army on the move.' (David Prior, *The Suffering and the Glory*)

U for unity: Agree with Paul that this is all about teamwork (verse 13a). Ask if we are really moving forward together.

> **Quote:** 'Like a mighty tortoise moves the church of God.
> Brothers we are treading where we've always trod.
> We are all divided, many bodies we;
> Strong in faith and doctrine, weak in charity.'
> (Anon)

Enthuse your church to be together, working with each other and encouraging – like the four men in Mark 2:1–4.

> **Quote:** 'Geese fly 71% further if together rather than alone.' (Pat MacMillan)

M for maturity: Explain that there is a point in all this! In fact, there are two:

1. **Built up** (verse 12). Use the second half of verse 13, saying how wonderful it would be if this became true for this church.

2. **Grown up.** Ask if we follow all the latest trends to the exclusion of whatever went before, or if we never move at all.

> **Quote:** 'Your church may be the happy-clappy or the frozen chosen.' (Jan Stafford of All Nations Christian College)

Emphasise the importance of our being Christian men and women, not immature children.

Ending: Ask, 'Where are you in all this?' Perhaps a quiet time for prayer and thought would be good, with verse 16 as our goal and Jesus doing it for us (verses 15b and 16a).

41. Communion/Eucharist

WHEN: Communion/Eucharistic service. Feast of St Thomas (July 3).

WHO: Seekers.

AIM: To use a remarkable African liturgy to encourage those who share in a Communion service to find a very special blessing as they participate. However, the talk will work in other services, too.

EXPLANATION: This talk is based on an ending to a Communion service in the new liturgy of the Anglican Church of Kenya (ACK). You may need the words on paper or screen to enable your congregation to share without trying to remember the words, although they are not difficult.

VISUAL AID: You will need a cross at the front of the church.

BIBLE READINGS: Luke 22:14–20; 1 Corinthians 11:17–34.

OUTLINE:
Introduction: Explain that you are all going to do something a little out of the ordinary today. At the end of the

service you are going to do what the ACK does: go out of church with a spring in your step. They have a response which you want everyone to join in, which goes like this:

> *Leader:*   All our problems
> *Everyone:* We send to the cross of Christ. [This is done with a sweep of the hand towards the cross by leader and congregation]
> *Leader:*   All our difficulties
> *Everyone:* We send to the cross of Christ. [As before]
> *Leader:*   All the devil's works
> *Everyone:* We send to the cross of Christ. [As before]
> *Leader:*   All our hopes
> *Everyone:* We set on the risen Christ. [This time with a sweep of the arm upwards to the ceiling]

Give a little demonstration (with a good, strong arm movement) as you say all this. It really does work! Now say that this ending is about four things:

All our problems: Talk about how we often feel we are failures, as in this sad quote:

> **Quote:** 'Life is all a failure in the end. The thing is to get sport out of trying.' (Sir Francis Chichester, round-the-world yachtsman)

Mention the burdens we carry – pain, poor health, wealth (whether we have it or not). Bring in the answer, using your favourite from Isaiah 53:4, Matthew 11:28 and 1 Peter 5:7. So, we can send 'all our problems . . . to the cross of Christ'.

All our difficulties: Here you could raise how we face the past and the future, our marriage or singleness or widow-hood, our careers, getting older, etc.

> **Quote/Story:** Frasier Crane, from the TV series *Frasier*, about to receive a lifetime achievement award, inter-views himself and says, 'I've achieved everything, and yet I'm completely empty.'

You could bring in the great words of Hebrews 13:5–6 as you repeat 'all our difficulties we send to the cross of Christ'.

All the devil's works: Say how we are reminded of our wrongdoings and failures at Communion services: Romans 7:21 works here.

> **Quote/Story:** In the re-make of the film *Alfie*, the film ends with Jude Law (Alfie) looking into the camera with these final words: 'I'm young. I'm single. I've got all I want. But I've not got peace of mind. And if you've not got peace of mind, you've got nothing.'

You could use Isaiah 53:5, so 'all the devil's works we send to the cross of Christ'.

All our hopes: The best comes last, you can say. Speak of all our futures, even death: God will be there with us.

> **Quotes:** 'There is a path in which every child of God is to walk, and in which God alone can accompany him.' (J. Denham Smith, *The Gospel in Hosea*)

> 'I know who holds the future
> And he holds me in his hand.'
> (From a song by Eugine I. Clark and Alfred B. Smith)

Ending: Simply say that we will all do the responses at the end of the service, after we have come to receive God's strength through bread and wine. Then do them just before the blessing.

42. Forgiveness

WHEN: Communion service. Second of four in Psalm 103 mini-series.

WHO: Men. Prisoners. This is a key talk for almost everybody.

AIM: To speak of how God forgives us.

THOUGHT: It is the author's experience that talks on forgiveness have a major impact on very many people: it is clearly a huge felt need today. (This talk can be used in conjunction with talk 43.)

BIBLE READING: Psalm 103:7–12.

OUTLINE:

Quote/Story: Some people can say exactly the right thing. Former Archbishop of Canterbury, Michael Ramsey, asked by a bright young student at a leading English university, 'What does Christianity have to offer a modern, technological society?' replied, 'The forgiveness of sins.'

Assuming 'nobody's perfect' (you could ask for any exception to identify themselves – seeking a second opinion from their partner. . .), you have amazing news from a man 3,000 years ago: David. (The reading could come here.) Run through these four headings:

God's problem: Verse 7a: the perfect creation has been spoiled. Give a couple of illustrations, one global, one local (the ozone layer, litter). Verse 7b: the Ten Commandments have not been kept, the perfect standard has not been achieved. God sees our failure.

God's character: Amazing verse 8. We get cross with those who offend us. God's nature is kindness and love.

> **Quote:** 'There is no sin which cannot be forgiven if we approach the throne of mercy with humble and contrite hearts.' (Pope John Paul II at Liverpool Cathedral, May 1982)

Because of who God is, we see

God's attitude: He sees our sins, knows we're wrong.

> **Quote:** 'There isn't anybody who doesn't regret their mistakes and wish they could re-wind the tape and run it again – but they can't.' (Kevin Maxwell, son of Robert Maxwell)

Contrast this with God and his approach in verses 9 and 10. He wants to forgive and restore. He wants a good, new relationship with us. This is because of

God's love: Verses 11 and 12. How has this become possible? Because God sent his own Son to live here and die on the cross.

Quote: 'Who delivered up Jesus to die? Not Judas, for money; not Pilate, for fear; not the Jews, for envy – but the Father, for love!' (Octavius Winslow)

Because God has raised Jesus, he is able to bring this forgiveness now. Our major sins, our minor sins, all our sins: we can have forgiveness.

Ending:

Quotes: 'The first anthem of the church is, "Kyrie eleison, Christe eleison, Kyrie eleison" – "Lord have mercy, Christ have mercy, Lord have mercy".' (Bishop Roy Williamson, *For Such a Time as This*)

'Belief in total, absolute forgiveness does not come readily.' (Henri Nouwen, *The Return of the Prodigal Son*)

Invite people to receive and know God's forgiveness.

43. Forgiveness

WHEN: Lent.

AIM: To take the 'other side of the coin' from talk 42, which deals with our being forgiven. This talk is about us forgiving others and is to enable forgiveness to be given, as well as received.

HINT: Talk 42 and this one might work well on consecutive weeks, possibly during Lent, when forgiveness has some priority.

BIBLE READING: Colossians 3:5–17.

OUTLINE:
Introduction: If you did use talk 42, say that this is part 2. Or you could say that there are some tough things we have to do in our lives. You could recall being told as a child to say 'Sorry' – the hardest word in the dictionary. But, as you have got older, you have found something harder – forgiving another's wrong against you.

> **Quote:** 'Real forgiveness means looking steadily at the sin, the sin that is left over without any excuse after all allowances have been made, and seeing it in all its horror, dirt, meanness and malice, and nevertheless being

wholly reconciled to the person who has done it. That, and only that, is forgiveness.' (C. S. Lewis)

Admit that such a quote is a shock and a challenge. Why should we forgive like that? And how can we?

For God's sake: This is the big one, you need to say. Give three pointers:

1. **God has forgiven us.** Colossians 3:13b is echoed in Ephesians 4:32. If you want to put a story into what could be a rather cerebral talk, the one Jesus told in Matthew 18:21–35 would work very well here. If you use it, you could have that as a second reading earlier in the meeting/service. We have sinned greatly against God and received unconditional forgiveness: that is our reason to forgive.

2. **God tells us to forgive.** Take your hearers to the Lord's Prayer in Matthew 5, drawing from verses 12 and 15, pointing out that this is the only conditional part of the whole prayer. Say how the bridge between us and God is broken or blocked through our unforgiving spirit.

   Quote: 'If you won't forgive, you can't be forgiven.' (Selwyn Hughes)

3. **We have God's nature.** 1 Corinthians 2:16 is good here. Draw from Psalm 103:8, 12. Then ask if we forgive like that. Suggest the sort of things we hear – 'Forgive – but can't forget' (do we want God to do that?); 'Forgive – but never speak to them' (should God do that with us?); 'Have nothing to do with them' (so we want God to

have nothing to do with us?). Now return to the Lord's Prayer: 'Forgive us . . . as we forgive'.

End this section with God's total forgiveness.

For our sake: Agree that this sounds selfish, but why should the offender win? Go to the reading at verse 15: isn't that what we want? Why should we carry the burden of an unforgiving heart?

> **Quotes:** 'An unforgiving heart holds resentment, and so carries with it resentment's poisonous effects.' (Selwyn Hughes)

> 'Do we accept the rejection of the world that imprisons us, or do we claim the freedom of the children of God?' (Henri Nouwen, *The Return of the Prodigal Son*)

Encourage your hearers to be set free.

For their sake: Agree that we are all failures who need to be free: set them free, even Christians.

> **Quote:** 'Christians are never perfect. They are simply those who recognise themselves as miserable sinners, ask for God's forgiveness and renewal, and thank him afterwards.' (Lord Brian Mawhinney, *In the Firing Line*)

Admit that this may not lead to reconciliation, as that is up to them. But mercy and grace can be given.

Ending: Be encouraging and upbeat: will your hearers, by a deliberate act of will and with God's help, forgive the one who has wronged them? Everyone – God, us, them – will win if they do.

44. Giving

WHEN: Financial appeal. Church anniversary service. Harvest.

AIM: To encourage Christians to give all they are and have to God, including their money.

EXPLANATION: This talk is a 'to the heart' presentation of seeing financial giving within the context of our entire lives being surrendered to God. Talk 45 is much more practical, with the mechanics explained, and deals more specifically with money.

BIBLE READING: 2 Corinthians 8:1–12.

OUTLINE:
Introduction: Say in a light-hearted way that you have drawn the short straw because, without putting too fine a point on it, you have to do the annual 'give us your money' talk!

> **Quote:** 'The last thing God is allowed to touch is a Christian's pocket.' (Neville Knox)

Here comes a very honest talk.

Christianity equals all I've got: Ask your hearers how involved they are in being Christians, using this famous quote:

> **Quote:** 'I was asked if I was still involved in tennis. I replied, "I've never been involved in tennis. I'm committed to tennis." It's the difference between the hen and the pig in eggs and bacon. The hen is involved, the pig is committed.' (Martina Navratilova)

You could ask your hearers if their financial giving comes from what they do or who they are. Say (if it is true) that when Jesus grabbed you, it meant giving all you had got.

> **Quote:** 'How easy it is for a poor man to depend on God! What else has he to depend on? And how hard it is for a rich man to depend on God! All his possessions cry out, "Depend on us!" ' (Rabbi Moshe Leib)

Why should we give all we have? Because

Christianity equals all Jesus has got: Turn to the reading, showing that Paul did not beat about the bush when explaining why the Corinthians should give. It was because Jesus had (verse 9). Help your hearers to understand that this is our only motivation: the greatest generosity encourages the greatest generosity. Jesus had everything, but gave it all away. His impoverished life and appalling death makes anything we do seem minimal.

You could go through some of the things Jesus had to borrow: the stable and the manger, the bread and the fish, the donkey, the Passover room, the tomb. Only the cross was his own. But it was really mine.

Which is why

Christianity equals all you've got: What we get from Jesus is amazing: give some of the best examples:

- Life itself (John 10:10). If we have not got this, we are still searching for the ultimate.

  Quote: 'The richest man in the world still needs something. No matter how rich you are, you still have something that you cannot get.' (The Sultan of Brunei, in conversation with Alan Whicker, 1992)

- Peace (John 12:27).
- Joy (John 15:11).

  Quote: 'How many millions does it take to satisfy a man? The next one.' (John D. Rockerfeller, when the world's richest man)

- Heaven (John 14:2).

Now put the challenge: how much shall we give in return? Answer: everything! Say that we will all have one regret in heaven (if regrets are allowed): that we had not given more.

Ending: Challenge your hearers to offer Jesus everything and then work out the money part of that.

45. Giving

WHEN: Financial appeal.

AIM: To give biblical guidance as to what we should give, to whom, and how to do it. This is a reasonably practical talk: talk 44 is more spiritual!

HINT: There is quite a lot in this, with many biblical references. You could even make it into a three-part mini-series. Otherwise, keep the talk moving.

BIBLE READING: Choose from Exodus 35:4–9, 20–22; Mark 12:38–44; 2 Corinthians 9:6–15.

OUTLINE:

Introduction: Start by saying that many of us would like a few practical tips about giving. Is it a tithe – a tenth – or what? Here are some pointers:

What should you give? The Bible speaks of at least six things:

1. **Yourself.** Point out that without this the rest is useless. Micah 6:6–8 works well here.

   Quote: 'Giving is a joy if we do it in the right spirit. It all depends on whether we think of it as "What can I spare?" or "What can I share?" ' (Esther Burkholder)

At this early stage in the talk, make the point that all the Old Testament sacrificial offerings ended with the sacrifice of Jesus: the only rule is in Romans 12:1. So what follows is only a guide.

2. **Your tithe.** Explain how this was the basic 'starter' for God's people (Leviticus 27:30–32): one tenth of net income. It's not a rule now – but should we give less than they did?

3. **Your first.** This was the 'first fruits' (Leviticus 23:10). Suggest that today's equivalent might be the increase in the pay rise the first time it happens. It shows God has our first.

4. **Your thanks** (Leviticus 7:12). Say how good it is to say 'thank you', recalling the most famous one of all – for a new baby (Leviticus 12:6). The poor Joseph and Mary could only afford the second option (Luke 2:24), but they did it. Ask if we ever say 'thank you' to God in a practical way.

5. **Your abundance.** Take your hearers to Deuteronomy 16:10–11, explaining that if the people were especially blessed they gave more.

6. **Your best.** Leviticus 1:3 and 3:1 show gifts 'without defect'. Malachi 3:8–10 can bring a big challenge to your hearers. Think what your best is for God.

To whom should you give? Ask your hearers: where is all this giving going? Four sources (you see how this could be part 2 of a mini-series).

1. **To God.** You could admit that this is stating the obvious,

showing that the very first offering was like this: Genesis 4:3. You could couple that with Noah in Genesis 8:20. If not to God, then the rest is useless.

2. **To the ministry.** If you are the minister, say that there is nothing personal in this! The tithe is brought to the church (Deuteronomy 12:5–6), for the workers (Deuteronomy 26:11). Paul is strong on this: you could refer to 1 Timothy 5:18.

3. **To the needy.** Deuteronomy 14:29 is very good: you could read it out, showing how blessings come when we give.

4. **To yourself.** Admit that this is a surprise! The Passover lamb was sacrificed – and then eaten (Exodus 12:8). God's people had their annual holiday paid for by their offerings: check out Deuteronomy 12:10–19 and 14:22–27 (they turned their offering into food and – yes – strong drink: it's all in these passages!). Maybe we would be more hospitable if we did this.

How to give:

1. **Privately.** Matthew 6:2–4 is helpful.

2. **Generously.** This is the Mark reading – a great story.

   Quote: 'The man who loves money is the man who has never grown up.' (Robert Lynd)

3. **Caringly.** Draw on the generosity of God's people giving to the needy and the possibility of your poorer church folk getting a much-needed family holiday.

4. Happily. This is the Corinthians reading. The word 'cheerful' in verse 7, you can point out, translates more like 'hilarious' in the original Greek!

Quote: 'He is no fool who gives what he cannot keep to gain what he cannot lose.' (Jim Elliot, missionary martyr to the Aucas in South America)

Ending: You could simply quote 2 Corinthians 9:7–8 because it is so encouraging.

46. Obedience

WHEN: General use.

WHO: New Christians.

AIM: To encourage Christians to build their Christian lives in the best possible way, by following Jesus' example.

HINT: The talk has this heading so you know its thrust, not so you use it in your publicity – it is not a popular theme! However, being a Christian means obeying Jesus. Hopefully, the wonderfully positive reading will give you all you need to be just that. Verses are from Philippians 2 (unless stated).

BIBLE READING: Philippians 2:1–18.

OUTLINE:
Introduction: Ask your hearers if they know the best way to live the Christian life. Tell them that the answer is obvious when you think about it: do it the Jesus way!

> **Quote:** 'What's good enough for Jesus is good enough for me.' (Barry Cooper)

Be like Jesus: Start this section by talking about how children all want to be like the current sports or pop sensation – as in the film title, *Bend it Like Beckham*. If we want to excel as Christians, we need to be like Jesus. Point out that this is not only a good idea, the Bible tells us to: verse 5. What did he do?

– Take verse 6 to show that his first move was not to hang on to what he'd got. Ask your hearers, lightly, how easy it is for them to be prised out of their favourite cosy chair.

– Verse 7 has the double stunner which you need to go to town on: how Jesus 'made himself nothing', which led to servanthood. You could quote his own words from Matthew 20:28. A good illustration here is the John 13:1–17 incident of washing the disciples' feet, using verse 13 as Jesus' enjoiner to his disciples – and us. Will your hearers go that far?

– Bring the good news from the end of verse 7 and the start of verse 8, showing how Jesus became one of us and so understands our joys and sorrows, pleasures and pains, and what obedience means.

– The rest of verse 8 should be shared with a sense of wonder and awe, explaining as best you can how Jesus went all the way to his appalling death. Emphasise the word 'obedient'. Ask if we will go to the limit to obey Jesus.

Quote: 'Never give in, never give in, never, never, never, never. Never yield to the apparently overwhelming might of the enemy.' (Winston Churchill)

Having given this great challenge, lift your hearers with verse 9: Jesus was exalted by God and he will honour us, too: you could use Paul's comment about himself in 2 Timothy 4:8. Say how we will be glad we kept on keeping on.

Be for Jesus: If we obey Jesus, why should we?

– **For our own sake.** Ask if verse 11 is true: of course it is! If we act obediently, our lives will be as they should be (verse 13). If Jesus is not Lord, then we get it wrong:

> **Quote:** 'Sin is man's determination to manage himself.' (Rudolf Bultmann)

– **For the world's sake.** Say how others are watching us (verse 15) and listening (verse 16). Show that Paul was willing to do this, even if it cost him his life (verse 17): ask who has the nerve to be like that today.

> **Quote:** 'Live close to God. Live close to people. Bring God and people together.' (Alan Godson)

Ending: Encourage your hearers, with Jesus as their great example, to live as obedient Christians. This final quote is lovely:

> **Quote:** 'If I climbed some great mountain, and looked over the wide lands, you know very well what I would see. Brigands on the high road, pirates on the seas, in the amphitheatres men murdered to please the applauding crowds, under all roofs misery and selfishness. It is a really bad world, Donatus, an incredibly bad world. Yet in the midst of it I have found a quiet and holy people. They have discovered a joy which is a thousand times better than any pleasures of this sinful life. They are despised

and persecuted, but they care not. They have overcome
the world. These people, Donatus, are the Christians –
and I am one of them.' (Cyprian, first century)

47. Sharing with Other Faiths

WHEN: Faith-learning situation. Ascension Day. 'Tricky Questions' session.

AIM: To help Christians share their faith with those of other faiths in a sensitive, caring way.

HINT: This is a seriously tricky subject in these days of hyper-sensitivity in any approach to other faiths – though not perceived as such a problem in many countries where other faiths predominate. Try to strike the balance between doing nothing and over-aggression.

BIBLE READINGS: John 10:11–18; Acts 1:1–9.

OUTLINE:
Introduction:

> **Quote/Story:** You could joke about the 1662 Book of Common Prayer: the only time it mentions 'Evangelism' is in the Third Collect for Good Friday, where it prays for the conversion of 'Jews, Infidels and Turks'!

Ask if, and how, we should approach those of other faiths with the Christian message: you have four 'Ps' to help.

Principles (and **Privileges** – that makes five!): Try to show the universality of God's love in sending Jesus, using the great John 3:16. You can bring in the Ascension Day commission from Acts 1:8 and Matthew 28:19, plus John 10:16. Jesus loves everyone and died for all.

> **Quote:** 'The women stumbled over an event which has blown history open and which impels the church into the world to preach Christ crucified, and raised from the dead to new and eternal life.' (*The Times*, editorial, Good Friday 2000)

Problems: Explain that we are not to be spoiling for a fight. If necessary, we should apologise for ancient and modern conflicts.

> **Quote:** 'The Crusaders conquered Jerusalem and found in the end that Christ was not there. They had lost him through the very spirit and methods by which they sought to serve him. Many more modern and more refined crusaders end in that same barrenness of victory.' (Dr Stanley James, quoted by John Stott, *Christian Mission in the Modern World*)

Say that there are clear areas of disagreement; these are best avoided in any opening conversation – for example, Jesus being God, or his having to die.

Practicalities: Encourage your hearers to have a loving, caring style, attracting rather than arguing. As in Christianity, many members of other faiths are 'nominal', their religion being cultural and their knowledge of their faith limited. They are as confused as nominal Christians.

Quote: 'The theological porridge they are making.' (John Haines)

Speak of the need for quiet patience as relationships develop: we want people to know Jesus.

Quotes: 'It is as absurd to argue men into faith as it is to torture them.' (Cardinal John Henry Newman)

'Christianity does not mean arguing about Jesus: it means meeting Jesus.' (William Barclay)

This leads to our having great respect, not putting a person or their faith down. We should pray, and believe.

Positives: Here are a few for us to share:

1. **Jesus.** He is universally attractive. Show his character and the wonderful things he said and did.

2. **Forgiveness.** Get your hearers to share their own stories, especially about knowing that God has forgiven them. In most other faiths it is all but impossible for this to happen.

3. **Justice.** Suggest the use of the story in Luke 18:9–14. A fair God is intriguing!

4. **Action.** Highlighting the deeds of Jesus – healing, caring, righting wrongs – is an excellent approach.

5. **Grace.** The attitude of Jesus to Zacchaeus (Luke 19:1–10) and the woman taken in adultery (John 12:1–11) and the story of the prodigal son (Luke 15:11–32) show an amazing love: very much valued as a concept.

Quote: 'Each of us is an invited guest.' (John Sentamu, Archbishop of York)

Ending: Try to get your hearers to go, with prayer and love, to their neighbours who have another faith, to share Jesus with them.

48. Praise

WHEN: Praise service. Songs of Praise event. Last in mini-series on Psalm 103.

WHO: New Christians.

AIM: To enthuse your hearers to praise God and to explain why we do this.

HINT: This is an enthusing talk, so you will need to be up for it yourself! If you have been following the mini-series, you will want to draw on the rest of Psalm 103 for further reasons for praise, as well as those set out here.

BIBLE READING: Psalm 103:19–22.

OUTLINE: Other people seem full of praise for God. East Africans are full of 'Bwana asifiwe!' ('Praise the Lord!' in Swahili). Certain denominations go in for this sort of thing – why don't we? If yours is a church that does a lot of praising, explain that you are going to look at why you do this and what it should mean. If yours is not that sort of church, say that you hope to persuade them – and why. Here are the reasons David gives:

God is great: Show how it is often our pride or our embarrassment, or our not being used to saying nice things, which gives us the problem of praise. Then use verse 19 to speak of how great God is compared with anyone else.

Speak of how you personally never have a problem bowing the knee to God, the Father of our Lord Jesus Christ. No one has done so much, or given so much: bring in creation, the cross, the resurrection and heaven. This unique King of all is worthy of praise.

God is praised: Show from the first parts of verses 20 and 21 and all of verse 22 that everyone else is already praising God. Like them, we can direct ourselves towards God.

Quote: 'To worship is to quicken the conscience by the holiness of God, to feed the mind with the truth of God, to purge the imagination by the beauty of God, to open the heart to the love of God, to devote the will to the purpose of God.' (Archbishop William Temple)

As we worship, we are part of what heaven and creation are already doing: underline again the first half of those verses.

Quote: 'When the sun rises, do you not see a round disc of fire somewhat like a guinea? Oh, no, no; I see an innumerable company of the heavenly host crying, "Holy, holy, holy is the Lord God Almighty". ' (William Blake)

Whatever we do, those holier than ourselves praise God.

God is served: Here is the second half of verses 20 and 21. Praise leads to service.

Quote: 'To live with the hope of heaven enables one to

be among the world's most useful servants.' (Geoffrey Paul)

If our praise is just something we do in church and in praise meetings with other Christians, it's not the real thing. Are we 'too heavenly minded'?

God is – mine? Psalm 103 opens and closes with the same words; are they true? Everyone else is doing their praising: what about me?

> **Quote/Story:** Bart Simpson comes home with a survey for his dad Homer. 'What religion are you?' he asks. Homer replies, 'You know, the one with all the well-meaning rules that don't work out in real life – Christianity.' (From *The Simpsons*: TV cartoon series)

It is time to hand over our inhibitions and our lack of enthusiasm and go for it.

Ending: You could take your hearers right back to the intimacy of verse 1, with a time for prayer before a great song of praise to end.

49. Praise

WHEN: Praise service. Songs of Praise event.

AIM: This talk gives a more Christ-centred, New Testament view of praise than talk 48, hopefully giving a balance when both are used. The aim is to encourage people to praise the name of Jesus.

HINT: It would be good to have a couple of praise songs or hymns to fit in with the emphasis you feel right to place on this talk. The choice is legion!

BIBLE READING: Hebrews 13:8–16.

OUTLINE:

Introduction: You could begin by saying that as we are having a Songs of Praise/a service with praise hymns/a time of praise and worship, you thought you'd try to speak about what it all means – so here goes:

The cause of praise: Say that the reason we praise has an easy answer: Jesus. Start at verse 8 to show his being eternal, completely reliable whenever: make something great of this famous verse. Then move to verse 12, showing how our supreme cause of praise is his giving of his life-blood and how we praise him for his amazing sacrificial death.

> **Quote:** 'This is the mystery which is rich in divine grace unto sinners: wherein, by a wonderful exchange, our sins are no longer ours but Christ's, and the righteousness of Christ is not Christ's but ours. He has emptied himself of his righteousness that he might clothe us in it, and fill us with it; and he has taken our evils upon himself that he might deliver us from them.' (Martin Luther)

Say that we praise God because of Jesus, our cause of praise. But there is:

The cost of praise: Ask your hearers if they realise that praise is costly. Go to verse 12, explaining how Jesus went outside the conventions of his day – even to the rubbish tip (verse 11b). Now we join him (verse 13). It is worth pointing out that it cost him his life, whereas our praise will, at most, incur an occasional snide remark. It may also mean working through any negative emotions or inertia on our part.

> **Quote:** 'Carrying the sins of the world is of a different order to the pains of discipleship.' (Colin Bennetts, Bishop of Coventry)

Verse 14 is worth a mention, saying that the Hebrews (recipients of this letter) ended up without their city (Jerusalem). Ask if we are too reliant on our 'city' (Rome, Canterbury, Geneva, our own specific church-base) or if we are looking for 'the city to come'.

The call of praise: Show how verse 15 says, 'Let's get on with it!' Draw out 'through Jesus . . . to God' from that verse, as well as 'continually': ask, 'Do we?'

Quote: 'We worship, not because worship benefits us (although it does), not because we need to (although we do), nor because it is relevant to our lives (although it is), but because God is.' (Richard Neuhaus)

The concern of praise: Take your hearers from the 'sacrifice' in verse 15 to the sacrifices we must make if our praise is to be real. You could refer back to verses 1 to 3 and the care we should show others.

Quote: 'Whatsoever is done of love, be it ever so little and contemptible in the sight of the world, becomes wholly fruitful. For God weighs more the love out of which man works than the work which he does. He does much who loves much. He who has true and perfect love seeks himself in nothing, but only desires in all things to glorify God.' (Thomas à Kempis)

Ask if we love like that and if our praise leads us to action.

Ending: A pause for prayer, to get our lives right for praise, would lead to one or two rousing songs or hymns of praise.

50. Prayer

WHEN: Family service.

AIM: To encourage grateful prayer and to help praying become effective.

HINT: This talk is a gentle walk through a delightful incident in the life of Jesus. People often find prayer difficult: this talk should therefore be given simply and positively – which is why it would work with children.

BIBLE READING: Luke 17:11–19.

OUTLINE:
Introduction: You may want to do a bit of background reading on why leprosy was such a problem: Leviticus 13 and 14 help, with Leviticus 13:45–46 being central. This could give you a starter, as you say how Jesus met ten people with a serious disease who asked for his help.

The alternative is to admit how hard you find prayer sometimes, and that you have found a great story which helps you. Remind your hearers that small children find praying much easier, and how we need to rediscover a simple, trusting style.

Quote: 'Where are those ardent prayers?' (Leo Tolstoy,

writing of his praying as a child, in *Childhood Boyhood and Youth*)

Tell the story as it happens, bringing it to life, stopping to make the following points as to how the lepers prayed:

They prayed with respect: 'They stood at a distance' (verse 12). They called, 'Jesus, Master. . .'
You could draw from the Lord's Prayer, showing the balance between 'Our Father' and 'hallowed be your name' (Matthew 6:9). Congratulate these people for getting the right balance between being personal and being respectful. There is the beauty and love in 'Jesus', with the recognition of his position and authority of 'Master'.
Ask your hearers if their approach holds this balance in the confidence of a child, with politeness to the God of eternity.

They prayed without conditions: 'Have pity on us' (verse 12).

> **Quote:** 'We ought to act with God in the greatest simplicity, speaking to him frankly and plainly and imploring his assistance in our affairs just as they happen.' (Brother Lawrence, *The Practice of the Presence of God*)

Try to evoke the passion of these desperate people (although traditionally ten men, there is nothing to suggest some were not women). Show their lack of 'If you do this, then. . .'. They knew they deserved nothing: 'pity' indicates their recognition of this fact. It is a straightforward 'Help!' whatever the outcome.

> **Quote:** 'We need both his "Yes" and "No" answers if our faith is to grow.' (Oliver Howarth)

They prayed with faith: You will want to speak of the wonderful reaction of Jesus in verse 14, but it is what the lepers did in that verse which matters for this talk. They went, and were 'cleansed' as they did: hence the last words of verse 19.

> **Quote:** 'Prayer is the key that opens wide the inexhaustible storehouses of divine grace and power.' (Dr R. A. Torrey)

You could take the old adage 'seeing is believing', and say that in prayer it is the other way round. Ask your hearers if they believe that God does answer prayer, including theirs.

One prayed with thanks: The incident is primarily famous for the one who came back. It is especially popular with children: the 'loud' way he did it is excellent (verse 15)!

> **Quote/Story:** Candide meets an old man in Eldorado, the perfect city, and asks how prayers were offered to God. 'We never pray, we have nothing to ask of God, since he has given us everything we need. But we thank him unceasingly.' (Voltaire, *Candide*)

You could share also from Philippians 4:6, especially 'with thanksgiving'.

Ending: Enthuse your hearers to imitate the lepers – especially the thankful one – in their prayer lives.

> **Quote:** 'If we spend sixteen hours a day dealing with tangible things and only five minutes a day alone with God, is it any wonder that tangible things are 200 times more real to us than God?' (Dean William Inge)

51. Prayer

WHEN: General use.

AIM: To encourage persistence in prayer and to help your hearers see the huge value in praying.

HINT: This talk is an exposition of the reading. It needs to be given with a passion for prayer. Any church could be revolutionised by enthusiastic, believing, constant prayer.

BIBLE READING: Colossians 1:9–14.

OUTLINE:

Introduction: You could ask these opening questions: 'Does anybody pray for you?' and 'Do you pray for any-body?' An opening like this not only catches the attention, it gets you to where you want to be immediately. Then quote the first half of verse 9. How was Paul praying – and how can we?

Praying onwards: This is verses 9 and 10. Try to capture Paul's love for his readers and his wonderful hopes for them. Ask whom we pray for like this, bringing down God's blessings for others.

  Quote/Story: St Cuthbert saved a village from fire. He

said, 'God's power is always mightier than man's efforts. When we pray, strange powers are set at work; and when we do not pray we hinder those powers. There are times when we must fight fire with fire. In these dark days we are called to be the fire in the north.' (Gordon Bates, Bishop of Whitby)

Show that just as babies and children grow slowly but surely, Paul is anticipating steady growth (verse 10) as he keeps on praying. Ask if that is our style.

Praying forwards: Verse 11 takes the previous point a step further, being realistic about the pain and hurt we share with others who suffer. Share the fact that prayer is costly, to us as we pray and for others in their needs.

> **Quote:** 'Our most pressing need is a revival of intercessory prayer. Prayer that is strong, prevailing, believing, God-moving, hell-defeating, Christ-exalting, worker-producing and money-raising. Prayer that takes all we have and are, to offer it to God, as it took all that Jesus had, on Calvary, to give us the right to pray.' (Dr Sidlow Baxter)

Ask if we have got too busy in our lives, so prayer is squeezed out: people need our prayers.

Praying upwards: Take your hearers on to verse 12, showing how prayer includes thanking God for all he is doing. Prayer acknowledges that he is doing what we can't do.

> **Quote:** 'Prayer is God's work – it is something he does.' (Delia Smith at the National Prayer Breakfast, 1990)

Speak of Paul's confidence in a God who hears, cares and answers, asking if we have the same approach.

Praying inwards: Moving to verses 13 and 14, show how we are reminded about those who need to know God's help in their own lives, including ourselves. Ask if we have the experience of these amazing words. If we have, are we praying for others to experience them?

Quotes/Stories: St Monica is famous for only one thing. For 32 years she mourned and prayed for her godless, wayward son to be converted. Her son's name? St Augustine, one of the greatest church leaders ever.

Asked for the reasons behind his successful evangelism, Billy Graham said, 'There are three: prayer, prayer, prayer.'

Ending: Urge your hearers to be like Paul, with his passion for his readers.

Quotes: 'The two greatest difficulties in prayer are getting to it and keeping at it.' (Peter Barber)

'Prayer does not need proof, it needs practice.' (Pastor Billy Kim of South Korea)

You could take your hearers back to the key words of the whole reading, 'We have not stopped praying for you' (verse 9).

52. Sin

WHEN: Lent. Men's meetings. General use.

AIM: It is scary how many 'good' people get their lives horribly wrong – even those of us who preach. This talk is a 'health warning' to encourage even the best to stick in close to God and not drift away to disaster. Just once in a while it needs to be given.

HINT: Treat this seriously, but be very sure to end on a high note of hope. Work your way through the story of Cain from the reading, but end elsewhere.

BIBLE READING: Genesis 4:1–16.

OUTLINE:

Introduction: Ask, 'Do you think we ever learn from our mistakes?' Then ask, 'Can we ever learn from other people's mistakes?' You could give a couple of examples (King Canute trying to stop the waves would be one). Say how there is one man you'd like to talk about today who got pretty much everything wrong: Cain.

His desire was wrong: Cain is only in the Bible a few times – take your hearers to 1 John 3:12, which puts the story in a nutshell and states the problem. How like his father!

> **Quote:** 'Adam took the whole handbook and threw it over the hedge.' (Ivan Richardson)

Ask if your hearers are allowing evil to win, or if they have come to the cross of Jesus to be forgiven.

His decision was wrong: Cain brought something (verse 3), but Abel brought the first and best (verse 4). Explain that this is not fruit versus animal, but Abel brought what God wanted (check another Cain reference in Hebrews 11:4).

> **Quote:** 'Sin is man's determination to manage himself.' (Rudolf Bultmann)

Say how God cannot accept what we do if it does not come from what we are. Ask if we are giving our best, from the love of our hearts.

His demeanour was wrong: Come to verse 5 to show Cain's reaction. Having got it wrong, he failed to correct things.

> **Quote:** 'I sometimes take out my sins, forgive myself them, and put them back again.' (Professor Stephen Leacock)

Ask your hearers if sin matters to them.

His deed was wrong: He couldn't hit God, so he hit his brother (verse 8). We can follow 'the way of Cain' (Jude 11): talk about our impurity, anger, jealousy and so on. God warns us, as verse 7 shows (this is the first reference to 'sin' in the Bible).

His denial was wrong: Speak of the famous question from Cain in verse 9, emphasising that the answer to it is, 'No, you're not his keeper; you're his brother!'

> **Quote:** 'There are only two kinds of people – the righteous who believe themselves sinners; the rest, sinners who believe themselves righteous.' (Blaise Pascal)

Point out that, whomever else he fooled, Cain could never fool God.

His destiny was wrong: Verses 11 and 16 are a tragic end.

> **Quotes:** 'When you've run the gamut of experience, eaten all the forbidden fruits and found their sweetness can turn sickly sour on the tongue, what's left?' (Marianne Faithfull, singer)

> 'We are prisoners of our own selfishness.' (Confession at St John's, Westwood, Coventry)

Ending: Don't miss this! The 'Ds' of Cain (all the headings were Ds) stand for Dunce (or Duh-brain) in the corner: to encourage the rest of us not to go there. The key for you now is Romans 15:4. Say how Cain is a big warning to us all, who also get it wrong. You will find Psalm 51:17 gives a way out. Tell your hearers to stick close to Jesus. God does accept our sacrifice – as he did Abel's. Encourage your hearers to have hearts and lives acceptable to God.

53. Suffering

WHEN: 'Tricky Questions' session. Bereavement. Hard times. Remembrance Sunday.

AIM: To try to explain the problem of suffering. To help people see God's love for us as we struggle with the burdens of life.

HINT: This is one of the ultimate difficult subjects. You will need time to give this talk. Give it with concern and humility: you do not have all the answers.

BIBLE READING: Romans 8:18–25.

OUTLINE:
Introduction: You could hit this on the nose: 'If God is a God of love, why is there all the suffering in the world? Why do babies die, parents get cancer, countries starve? What's wrong with the world?' When you've done that, say that you will need more than five minutes, but you will do your best.

Back at the start: It would be good to read out Genesis 1:26–28, showing how we human beings are to 'rule over' the whole world and everything in it, followed by Genesis

2:15, to 'care'. Point out that the world is God's by creation, but ours by gift.

Move rapidly through Genesis 2:17, with its simple rule ('you must not eat'), to Genesis 3:6, when they did eat, leading to Genesis 3:17–18, where the 'curse' was 'because of you'. Our fall brought the whole structure down. You could use an illustration of carrying a precious vase: if you fall, the vase breaks as well.

> **Quote:** 'Ring-a-ring o'roses,
> A pocket full of posies,
> A-tishoo! A-tishoo!
> We all fall down.'
> (Kate Greenaway, from *Mother Goose*, 1881: although possibly originally from the time of the Black Death, fourteenth century)

Explain that the 'prince of this world' is at work (Jesus refers to him three times in John 12:31, 14:30 and 16:11). Check also Ephesians 2:2, and the cosmic struggle in Ephesians 6:12.

Forward to today: Here is a long quote, but a brilliant comment on the reading.

> **Quote:** 'In exact proportion to his "progress", "culture", "civilisation", man has become a devouring force before whose onslaught nature has wilted. During three to ten centuries nature can build an inch of fertile topsoil. During one reckless century man has used up, over vital areas of the world's surface, all nature's stored resources. Greedy farming and selfish exploitation has taken no

thought for the morrow. Hence bared hills, choked streams, dust-bowls, famine, disaster, polluted air, fouled rivers and dead lakes, as nature answers back . . . Man fell, and from his fall came his pain, his toil, his exile.' (Prof. E. M. Blaiklock, from *Scripture Union Bible Study Books – Romans*).

Bring in Romans 8:22–23, saying how it is often the 'innocent' who get hurt: all of us.

Quote: 'There is a broken heart in every pew.' (Joseph Parker)

Admit the truth that. . .

– We could spend our vast defence budgets on finding cures for most diseases
– That would mean no more war
– Then we could feed the starving
– And move those in flood areas to safer living.

There is hope: Turn to the positive. Take the first verses of the reading's chapter: Romans 8:1–2, with those further on: Romans 8:28, 37–39.

Quote: 'God whispers in our pleasures, speaks to our conscience and shouts in our pain.' (C. S. Lewis)

There is hope for the world: Isaiah 35:1–2.

Quote: 'The world is God's world and God will yet be glorified by all his works. And when God is glorified, his creatures are blessed.' (Prof. F. F. Bruce)

Point out that the Fall will not win in the end: Isaiah 11:6–9, Revelation 22:3. We should lift up our heads (Luke

21:28). We're on our way to complete victory, but we're not there yet.

Ending: Bring your hearers to the cross of Jesus, where evil was defeated and the Fall paid for. Help them to know the resurrection victory of Jesus, with the Holy Spirit's help (Romans 8:26).

TRICKY QUESTIONS

54. Who is God?

WHEN: 'Tricky Questions' session.

WHO: Young people. New Christians.

AIM: To answer the tricky question about who God is.

HINT: Many churchgoers and Christians need to know why they believe what they believe, so this would be good at any time. In a non-church setting, the readings are a guide only.

BIBLE READINGS: Isaiah 40:12–31; Ephesians 2:1–7.

OUTLINE:
Introduction: You could say that, of all the topics you will ever preach on, this is the biggest! You want to answer the question 'Who is God?' with three Ms.

Mighty God: That is Isaiah 9:6. It is worth making three points under this heading.

1. **Creator.** Draw from Genesis 1:1–3 and John 1:3. God is the great Creator.

   Quote: 'Seeing the immense design of the world, one

image of wonder mirrored by another image of wonder; the pattern of fern and feather echoed by the frost on the windowpane, the six rays of the snowflake mirrored by the rock-crystal's six-rayed eternity: I ask myself, "Were those shapes moulded by blindness?" Who, then, shall teach me to doubt?' (Dame Edith Sitwell, actress)

Show God's uniqueness: Isaiah 45:18 is good. Speak of his wonderful creativity: Isaiah 40:12. And he keeps the show going: Hebrews 1:3.

Quote: 'God is not stuck in a rut. He is marvellously creative.' (David Fewster)

2. **Greater than humans.** You can use the Isaiah reading again, at verses 13–14, plus Isaiah 55:8–9. Romans 11:33–36 is a good New Testament help.

Quote: 'God is God – and he's not applying for the job.' (Revd Steve Tash)

3. **The only God** (Isaiah 44:6–7). Ask if we are careful not to fall into the trap of Isaiah 40:18–20, even if our modern equivalents are shopped for!

Majestic God: Psalm 8:1 would give you this word.

Quote: 'We can never have too big a conception of God.' (J. B. Phillips, *Your God Is Too Small*)

Return to Isaiah 40, at verse 15, to show God's majesty over all other majesties. You could even point out that most of Isaiah's prophecy demonstrates this authority over the super-powers of the day: Babylon (13:1), Moab (15:1),

Damascus (17:1), Ethiopia (18:1), Egypt (19:1), Arabia (21:13), Tyre (23:1). Ask if your hearers believe this majesty still applies today – because it does (26:21). You could also draw on God's ultimate control, as over the world leader Cyrus (45:1). Do we let him control our lives?

> **Quote:** 'The Kingdom of God is not a democracy. The Lord never seeks re-election.' (Eric Liddell's father, as spoken in the film *Chariots of Fire*)

Now you have spoken of God's greatness, with people like 'grasshoppers' (Isaiah 40:22), come to your amazing third 'M':

My God: This is verses 27–31: capture the wonder of these. What an amazing relationship! The Ephesians reading fits here, especially from verse 4 onwards. Speak of our being raised up to God, to know him. Explain how we can experience this because of Matthew 27:46, where 'My God' is said, leading to Galatians 2:20. If you stick with Isaiah, 43:1 works well.

> **Quote:** 'For years I had instructed students on the different aspects of the spiritual life, trying to help them see the importance of living it. But had I, myself, really ever dared to step into the centre, kneel down, and let myself be held by a forgiving God?' (Henri Nouwen, *The Return of the Prodigal Son*)

You could use Isaiah 40:31 as a challenge, backed by 45:22 or 55:6–7 as well.

Ending: Here is part of a prayer which is sometimes used at the induction of clergy:

Quote: 'May the love of the Father enfold you, the wisdom of the Son enlighten you and the fire of the Spirit enflame you.' (Ministers' Induction Services, Diocese of Coventry)

55. 'I Did it My Way'

WHEN: 'Tricky Questions' session. Baptism.

AIM: To show that if we do things 'our way', we will not get to God. We must go his way.

HINT: This is very much a Scripture-based talk, being a walk-through of the passage. You would benefit from knowing the verses really well, because they speak for themselves. This is a talk in favour of God's grace and against the song's words, 'I did it my way'. The more 'churchy' your hearers, the more 'upright' they try to be, the harder will be the giving and receiving of this talk.

BIBLE READING: Ephesians 2:1–10.

OUTLINE:
Introduction: You could use a shock opening, along the lines of 'To be a Christian is not natural'! The point is that if we are ever to be true Christians, God must do it. Paul proves it in one sentence: the whole of Ephesians 2:1–10 is a single sentence in the original. Happily, the translators have given us pauses for breath.

Paul gives us the vast contrast between us and God:

Us: 'As for you' (verse 1). What we do is described in three words: 'dead', 'transgressions' ('trespasses', RSV), 'sins'.

– 'Dead.' There is nothing we can do: we need the kiss of life. So our good works, church-going and so on are of no value when done by dead people.
– 'Transgressions.' The original meaning is of aiming at a target and missing: we want to get things right but we don't achieve our goal.
– 'Sins.' Again, the original has the idea of walking along a path and falling off into a ditch.

Quote/Story: Lord Cecil was a former Bishop of Exeter. He was notoriously absent-minded. On a train journey, the inspector asked to see his ticket. When he failed to find it, the inspector, knowing him well, told him, 'Never mind.' Cecil replied, 'Oh, but it does matter – if I can't find my ticket, how am I to know where I'm going?'

Verses 2 and 3 underline the sinfulness of our lives. When we try to be good we are not showing the whole truth about ourselves.

Quote: 'We are all actors. Practically no social behaviour is "natural"! It is natural to rush and grab what we want like a baby or an animal. It is natural to growl and scream when our desire is thwarted, be it for a bone, a rattle or a bishopric.' (Actor, Sir Tyrone Guthrie, *On Acting*)

This is all of us: 'In our natural condition, we like the rest lay under the dreadful judgement of God' (verse 3, NEB).

Hooray for the contrast which follows:

God: 'But God' (verse 4). If we have messed things up, God has not.

> **Quote:** 'God does not play dice.' (Albert Einstein, in a letter to Max Born, 1926)

What is he like? Verse 4: 'Rich in mercy' and 'the great love with which he loved us'. Amazingly, despite our sin and need, he does not cast us away. Talk about the love of God, especially shown through Jesus on the cross.

God to us: Here comes the kiss of life: use verse 5. In his mercy, he forgives us.

> **Quote:** 'Forgiveness deals with the inexcusable and unjustifiable.' (C. S. Lewis)

We must let God come and breathe his new life into us.

Us to God: Verses 6 and 7 are even more remarkable. Here is such generosity. Two things are vital:

1. **God does it, not us.** Verses 8 and 9 are pivotal to understanding that grace means it is all of God. We must receive the 'grace of our Lord Jesus Christ' (2 Corinthians 13:14).

   > **Quote:** 'Salvation is ours, not by achieving, but by receiving.' (Dr R. P. Martin)

2. **A new life then begins.** Verse 10 shows that from the moment we receive God's grace, we then do live a godly life. 'Good works' do matter – but only when they flow from grace.

Ending: Receive God's free gift of grace!

56. What do We Believe?

WHEN: 'Tricky Questions' session. Church anniversary.

AIM: To encourage a genuine trust in the Lord by us all, especially those with doubts and questions.

HINT: Don't hang about with each point – unless you want to create your own mini-series out of this. There is certainly enough material for three or four talks. In giving this as one talk, give thumb-nail sketches of each heading. You may want to emphasise just one or two.

KEY: The very centre of the Bible is Psalm 118. There are 594 chapters before and after Psalm 118. The previous psalm is the shortest Bible chapter, the next is the longest (2 and 176 verses). Excepting Psalm 118, there are 1,188 chapters in the Bible. Taking those four digits (1188) we see that Psalm 118:8 says, 'It is better to trust in the Lord than to put confidence in man.' That's the secret, and the key verse.

Why do we need to do this? This psalm tells us all these things about God:

BIBLE READING: Psalm 118:1–14.

OUTLINE:

The Lord is good (verse 1): He is perfect and always gets it right, compared with trusting human beings (verse 8).

> **Quote:** 'The human reality is a flawed reality. We neither see clearly what the good is, nor do we have the strength to do it, having seen it.' (*The Times*, editorial, Ash Wednesday, 1998)

Why do we trust ourselves instead of the God whose 'love endures for ever'?

The Lord loves (verses 1–4): He loves us all. A good Bible quote is Lamentations 3:22–23, showing the constancy of God's love.

The Lord answers (verse 5): This would compare delightfully with the curse of voicemail!

> **Quote:** God is 'always more willing to hear than we are to pray'. (1662 Book of Common Prayer)

The Lord sets free (verse 5, second half): This would be a great time to speak of the death and resurrection of Jesus.

> **Quote/Story:** With the first half of verse 5: Michel Quoist, in his book *Meet Christ and Live*, has a chapter called 'The Age of Anguish': very appropriate for today's world.

The Lord is here ('with me', verses 6 and 7): Who else is there all the time? You could refer back to Psalm 23:4: even in the 'valley of the shadow of death'.

The Lord helps (verse 7): This is especially so in times of trouble. You could add the lovely promise of Isaiah 43:2, and compare with Psalm 118:8, when human beings often let us down, and verse 6, because the help gives protection.

The Lord strengthens (verse 14): Here is the power and joy of the Holy Spirit.

> **Quote:** 'This verse is written out of the experience of many who have first of all found the broken needs of the creature break under them, and have afterwards joyfully found the Lord to be a solid pillar sustaining all their weight.' (C. H. Spurgeon, *Selections from the Treasury of David*, writing about verse 8, with all that follows up to verse 14)

The Lord gives joy (verse 14, second half): Speak of how wonderful it is to know God's presence.

Ending: Back to the key verse: verse 8 says it all. So let's do it!

57. Do We All Go to Heaven?

WHEN: 'Tricky Questions' session.

AIM: This is a controversial talk, aiming to take the view Jesus took that not everyone goes to heaven, that 'universalism' is not true. It looks positively at how we do get to heaven and needs to be given in that way.

HINT: The old line of 'accentuate the positive' is key here. This is a vital subject and needs to be preached at some time in every church, because churchgoers need to know the way to heaven as much as anyone else.

BIBLE READING: Matthew 22:1–14.

OUTLINE:
Introduction: 'Aren't weddings great?' would be a good first line – it gets everyone's positive attention and gets you right to the story Jesus told. Say how Jesus enjoyed weddings (as with the one at Cana in John 2:1–11) and how he told a story about one.

A favour rejected: The first two verses speak of a great invitation. It would be good to talk about God's offer of forgiveness to us. You should speak of his offer of forgiveness and new life through the death and resurrection of his Son Jesus and how he now invites us to his feast in heaven.

Get to the tragedy of verse 3. You could point out that Jesus was partly using this story to show how the Jews were rejecting him (going to verse 6). But verse 5 is for us – what gets between us and our saying yes to God's free invitation of new life?

Quote: 'It is not the darkness that blocks your vision so much as what is between you and the Light.' (Gail Trafford)

Comment on the fact that Jesus does not say that what the people went to ('field', 'business') was wrong: but that anywhere other than the banquet was wrong.

Quote/Story: In the old TV series *Lou Grant*, about an American newspaper reporter, one story featured a Jewish boy who became a Nazi. A girl reporter met the rabbi who had taken the boy's Bar-mitzvah, asking if he was horrified. The rabbi replied: 'When you turn your back on God, whichever way you go it's the wrong direction.'

Point to Jesus not hiding the fate of the rejectors (verse 6).

A feast restored: Verses 8–10 are delightful: enthuse about God's generosity to us. All are invited. In verse 9, 'street corners' is also 'thoroughfares' in some translations. The Greek literally is 'exoduses': you could draw on how God is giving us a 'way out' from where we are to where he is.

There are some great words you could major on. 'Invite' is lovely – there is no coercion by God for us to respond. 'Both good and bad' (verse 10) means we are all welcome – and we all need to respond.

The word 'ready' in verse 8 is also key: it means we do not have to do anything but accept and come. This will give you the lead-in to the serious third factor:

A friend removed: The last four verses need to be tackled with honesty and concern.

> **Quote:** 'If we are saved, it is by grace alone. If we are disinherited, it is by our own choice.' (R. T. Kendall)

The 'wedding garment' is the king's gift. Ask your hearers what they plan to wear in heaven: joke about best suits/dresses. Then go to Revelation 7:13–14. Only the blood of Jesus makes our clothes clean enough.

Show that the guest seemed to have fooled everyone else – but the king noticed (verse 12). Ask if our good behaviour/church-going/position in society fools everyone, even ourselves. We may be a 'friend' (verse 12) yet be thrown out (verse 13). We will be 'speechless'.

Ending: Say that this is a story without a happy ending. Will we 'live happily ever after'? We need to get our wedding garment now – from the King. Let's not leave it too late.

> **Quote:** 'We've got to remember that we've only got one life to live. It's not a rehearsal.' (Dennis Thatcher, in his last-ever interview, 2003)

SPECIAL EVENTS

58. Adult Baptism

WHEN: Baptism. Easter.

WHO: New Christians.

AIM: To show how the Christian life means a total transformation of our lives.

HINT: If you are speaking at a baptism involving total immersion, use the visual aid right in front of you. Show how the going into the water is a picture of 'died' and the coming out is the 'raised' in what follows.

Remember that at most baptisms people who are from way outside the church are usually present – the family and friends of those being baptised. Keep your talk free of 'religious lingo' and explain what you are saying carefully.

BIBLE READING: Colossians 2:20 – 3:4.

OUTLINE:

Introduction: A dramatic introduction could be to open with: 'Christianity isn't reformation – it's revolution!' Say how you would like to show this by sharing three simple things about the baptism which follows, based on some words from the apostle Paul.

If this is a talk for a non-baptismal occasion, you are asking, 'What is a real Christian?' If this is for an adult baptism of a true believer, the question is, 'What are we seeing here today?'

Christians/baptised adults have:

Died with Christ: Colossians 2:20: 'You died with Christ'. Paul says this of himself in Galatians 2:20. What does this mean? Show how we need to acknowledge our sins and, by an act of will, turn our lives over to Christ, so our old lives die.

> **Quote:** 'Very often it is not intellectual difficulties, but failure to repent of sin that keeps people from seeing that Jesus is the Christ.' (David Gooding, *True to the Faith*)

This is a radical revolution – like death. We identify with the death of Jesus on the cross.

> **Quote:** 'Each individual gains salvation through a total interior renewal which the gospel calls "metanoia"; it is a radical conversion, a profound change of mind and heart.' (Pope Paul VI, *Evangelii Nuntiandi*)

Secondly, a Christian/baptised adult is:

Raised with Christ: 'You have been raised with Christ' (Colossians 3:1). This is a brand-new life – you could show the new outlook described in 3:2. A good comparison is with Matthew 6:31–33.

Everyone else is solely concerned with the affairs of this world, debilitating their lives. The revolution is to live the new life that Christ gives.

Quote: 'I am constantly struck by the fact that those who have learnt that there is nothing and nobody in this life to cling to, are the really creative people. They are free to move constantly away from the familiar, safe places and can keep moving forward to new, unexplored areas of life.' (Henri Nouwen)

We are meant to live our lives in glory, not the gutter. Show how the wonderful resurrection life of Jesus Christ is ours to live. We can do this because we are:

Hidden with Christ: 'Your life is now hidden with Christ in God' (Colossians 3:3).

Quote: 'Delia walks with God and isn't any more, because God has taken her.' (Delia Smith, speaking at the National Prayer Breakfast, November 1990, referring to Enoch in Genesis 5:24)

Say that a Christian is doubly safe, in the hands of Jesus and his Father: John 10:28–30 ('my hand . . . the Father's hand . . . I and the Father are one' – check the verses).

There is a heaven: 3:4. The Christian is safe for ever. With this protection, any hardship can be faced.

Ending: Enthuse those being baptised to believe this as they come to the water. Encourage everyone else to join the revolution: to die, to rise, to be safe.

59. Bereavement

WHEN: Times of bereavement. Memorial service. Funeral. Third in the mini-series on Psalm 103. Remembrance Sunday.

AIM: To bring comfort and encouragement to those who are suffering loss. This is primarily loss through the death of someone special, but it could include other serious times of loss, such as the loss of one's home (appropriate for those who have moved to residential care, for example).

HINT: As with all talks of this kind, the gentle way you deliver this will count for more than what you say. It is a great opportunity to bring God's love to the broken-hearted.

BIBLE READING: Psalm 103:13–18.

OUTLINE:
Way in: You could begin by saying that you don't know anyone who has never been hurt. As you get older, you are increasingly aware of people suffering loss and how, in such circumstances, we all need some help. Your big question is, 'Where is God in all this and can he help?'

Say how these few verses from King David tell us four things about God:

1. God loves us (read verse 13).

Quote: 'Brennan Manning tells the story of an Irish priest who, on a walking tour of a rural parish, sees an old peasant kneeling by the side of the road, praying. Impressed, the priest says to the man, "You must be very close to God." The peasant looks up from his prayers, thinks for a moment, and then smiles, "Yes, he's very fond of me".' (Philip Yancey, *What's So Amazing About Grace?*)

You need to be careful if someone has just lost a father, but you could point out that David's own father was not brilliant (not counting him among his sons when Samuel visited him in 1 Samuel 16:1–13). No – this is the Father of Jesus, who loves us with 'compassion'.

Quote: ' "Compassion": a deep feeling of pity for the suffering of another, and an inclination to give aid or support, or to show mercy.' (*Reader's Digest Universal Dictionary*)

God does care: but, also:

2. God knows us (verse 14). Show how God knows the hurts of the world and of each one of us, because Jesus came all the way to the 'dust' of the cross and the grave.

Quote: 'The Bible reveals a God who, while man is still shrouded in darkness and sunk in sin, takes the initiative, rises from his throne, lays aside his glory, and stoops to seek until he finds him.' (John Stott, *Basic Christianity*)

God's own Son was laid in the dust of death. However far away we feel from God, however hurt we are, God is here for us.

Quote: 'We can never be so damaged or so far away that God's love cannot reach us.' (Peter Findley)

3. God sees us (verses 15 and 16). Death reminds us of the brevity of life: we, too, are dying. Tell your hearers that what they feel is normal: tears, grief, anger, pain, hurt, guilt, depression: so they should not panic. Encourage them to accept the way they are and to know that God has given us these verses to show that he understands. But, in all this, the best is that:

4. God helps us (verses 17 and 18). Explain that these verses describe a love which is not here today and gone tomorrow. Tell how 'Jesus wept' (John 11:35), how God the Father was bereaved by the death of the one he loved most when Jesus died so horribly, and how Jesus himself gave his life for our own failures. Now he wants to help us with our grief. Will we let him?

Quote: 'A little step from us, a great step from him.' (Ivan Richardson)

Ending: If this is a funeral, leave it there. If you are speaking at a memorial service some distance in time from the death, you could encourage a more positive response, encouraging your hearers to let the truths of these verses be theirs. Many people do find real faith at times of loss and bereavement, so why not your hearers?

60. Funeral

WHEN: Funeral. Bereavement service. Songs of Praise event (with 'The Lord's My Shepherd'). Remembrance Sunday.

AIM: This will depend on the type of service or event: the above list shows a great variety of situations. Depending on the event, emphasise the appropriate verses in what follows. However, this is a great psalm of comfort and help, which is the main aim.

HINT: In any talk at a time of great sorrow, a gentle approach is vital. Bring God's love to broken hearts.

BIBLE READING: Psalm 23.

OUTLINE:
Introduction: There is a story of a preacher visiting the home of a farmer. He meets the farmer's son, who says he is the lad who tends the sheep. The preacher asks if he knows the Good Shepherd. The boy says 'No' and the preacher shares how he can know Jesus as his Saviour. Pointing to his hand, he counts from the thumb, 'The Lord is my Shepherd', clasping the ring finger for 'my'. 'Trust your life to Jesus, so you can say "my".'

In the winter, the boy goes to bring in the sheep from the hills. He is lost in a snowstorm. He is found dead in a drift, clutching his ring finger. He had trusted the Shepherd.

Do we know this Shepherd in our lives?

A relationship (verse 1a): You could mention some of the other titles the Psalms give to God ('King', 'Deliverer', 'Rock', 'Shield') and compare with the intimate 'Shepherd'. This is the Lord who cares deeply, who loves and embraces us.

> **Quote:** 'For me, the most profound truth of my faith is that there is someone who loves me completely and totally in spite of my weakness and failure.' (Cardinal Basil Hulme, just before he died)

This relationship is both personal ('my') and present ('is'). There is a great certainty which we can know: do we?

A refreshment (verse 1b): 'Not be in want'. Lead into verse 2, lying down in green pastures: sheep lie down when they are full. There is the togetherness of being led by 'quiet waters': the peaceful presence of the Holy Spirit.

A restoration (verse 3a): We all need to be brought back home from the hills where we have strayed. Gently encourage your hearers to know God's forgiveness through the death of the Shepherd for all his sheep (John 10:11). He can be there to restore us at our lowest moments.

> **Quote:** 'Faith, the dark night of the soul.' (Title of a poem by St John of the Cross)

A road (verse 3b): The Lord leads in the right way. His way is good, even if it sometimes feels otherwise.

You may want to major on verse 4. See how David moves from the third person ('He leads me') to the very personal second person ('You are with me'). The Lord is in there with him in 'the deepest darkness' (Good News Bible).

Quote: 'Whatever do people do without the Lord to depend on?' (Tony Nelson)

There is only a 'shadow' because there is the light of God's presence (John 8:12).

A reality: Verse 5 shows how the Shepherd is now a personal friend, meeting all our needs, leading to his caring for us both now and for ever (verse 6).

Ending: With all these 'Rs' for headings, we now need a response. This will depend on the occasion: it could be to trust the Shepherd, or to receive his comfort or leading as we follow him. Our hearers need to be encouraged to be 'up close and personal' with the Shepherd who loves them.

61. Children

WHEN: Family service. Harvest. Mother's Day.

AIM: To use the delightful story of the boy who gave his picnic to Jesus to show what a Christian is.

HINT: Make this incident live. It is full of action and excitement, but also gentleness and homely touches. The Colgate story is lovely, as everyone uses toothpaste!

VISUAL AID: Five bread rolls and a tin of sardines would work well. You will need a table and a knife to make sandwiches with them. Offer them to anyone at the end.

BIBLE READING: John 6:1–14.

OUTLINE:
Introduction: If you are using the visual aid, produce your rolls and sardine tin and say you have a picnic story as you start to prepare the sandwiches. If not (or even if you are), and you are with churchgoing children, you could ask which is the only miracle (apart from the resurrection) in all four Gospels (it's this one. . .). Or simply say you've got a great story to tell – a true one – about a boy. (Read the Bible reading.)

He followed Jesus: Say how children find that following Jesus is wonderful.

> **Quote:** 'The piper's calling you to join him.' (From the song 'Stairway to Heaven' by Led Zeppelin)

You could pick up on any of these points:

- He was only young: the Greek (verse 9) is *paidarion*, 'a little lad'. We can know Jesus when we are little.
- He was with others who followed Jesus (verse 2).
- He followed all day, to evening time (Matthew 14:15).
- He was keen – he 'ran' (Mark 6:33).
- He learned about God from Jesus (Luke 9:11).

You can talk about us doing these things, being keen to go with Jesus, learning from him.

> **Quote:** 'I cannot fail to be thrilled every time I read the things that Jesus said, and I am more and more convinced of the necessity of following him. What Jesus means to me is this: in him we are able to see God and to understand his feelings towards us. (Charles Schulz, creator of the 'Peanuts' cartoon strips)

He gave what he had: Come to verse 9, showing how his gift was not rich – the rolls were 'small' and 'barley' (a poor family's bread). But – make a big thing of this – Jesus took them gladly. He took all the boy had and the boy trusted Jesus with his whole picnic. He was willing: otherwise, how did Andrew know?

> **Quote/Story:** Many years ago, in America, a boy left home, knowing only how to make soap. He decided to be honest, and to give God a tenth of every dollar he earned.

He prospered and found he could give two tenths, then three, then four. Eventually he gave all his income to Christian work. He died immensely rich. He was – William Colgate.

Jesus blessed: Say how there were three blessings:

1. **For the gift.** It would be good to use Matthew 14:19. Share with your hearers that whatever we give to Jesus, however ordinary and humble, he will receive and bless.

2. **For others.** Pick up on the words used in the different accounts: everyone got a blessing ('all' Mark 6:42), and was 'satisfied' (Matthew 14:20). Draw out that when we give to Jesus he can do wonders for others.

   Quote: 'It was as if the whole universe came from his hands.' (Oliver Howarth, commenting on this miracle)

3. **For the boy.** He shared the feast. You could joke about boys having bottomless pits for stomachs, but there were still basketfuls left (verse 13). He didn't lose out.

   Quote: 'Jesus gives a super-abundance of life: it comes from the Latin meaning "the crest of the wave". We are to be on the top of the wave.' (John Sentamu, when Bishop of Birmingham)

Ending: Enthuse your hearers, however young, to delight in going with Jesus, giving him their love and their lives.

62. Healing Service

WHEN: Healing service. First in mini-series on Psalm 103. Communion/Eucharist.

WHO: Older people.

AIM: To bring God's healing: but within the context of God wanting to reach into every part of our lives.

EXPLANATION: This is the first of four talks based on Psalm 103, so it can be used at any time: see talks 42, 59 and 48 for the others, in that order. However, each talk stands on its own and this one can be used for any situation of need.

HINTS: With any talk when those present have perceived problems, be gentle in your approach, while not understating your hearers' need to let God help them.

There are a lot of points: don't linger too long on each.

BIBLE READING: Psalm 103:1–6.

OUTLINE:
Introduction: Talk a little of the problems we gather through life. We do wrong things, our lives get in a mess,

we get ill in body and mind. Say how we need love and kindness. These are not problems to God, because he has the answers.

Who is God? Explain that you are simply going to walk through the verses you have read from Psalm 103, beginning with verse 1. God is 'the Lord': the God of creation, the God of eternity, full of 'righteousness and justice' (verse 6). And yet – we can know him in 'my soul'.

> **Quote:** 'God is holy, but wholly available.' (Geoff Walton)

Where does he come? Quote the second half of verse 1. We often think we have to reach out to God. But he is there, waiting for us.

> **Quote/Story:** There is a Chinese fable of a weary desert traveller, who finally reaches the shade of a great tree. 'How lucky I am to have found you!' 'Lucky?' replies the tree, 'It's not luck. I've been waiting here for 700 years!' (From Richard Bewes, former Rector of All Souls, Langham Place, London)

God waits for us: are your hearers coming to him?

What does he do?

1. He forgives (verse 3a). Whatever our other needs, explain how we all need this. We all must come to the cross of Jesus.

> **Quote:** 'We may note the irony that in our secular world dieting comes in where religious fasting goes out,

and counselling and therapy burgeon where men and women avoid confession of sin and the acknowledgement of their need for forgiveness.' (*The Times*, editorial, Ash Wednesday, 25.2.98)

2. He heals (verse 3b). Show how this follows forgiveness. Quote the end of Exodus 15:26 – 'I am the Lord who heals you.' God, by his Spirit, wants to touch our lives.

3. He redeems (verse 4a). You could refer to the echo of this in Psalm 40:2. Show how this is the follow-on from the previous two points – the sense of being brought back, rescued.

4. He crowns (verse 4b). Explain how God wants to lift us to a place of honour. You could speak of what a lovely word 'compassion' is – the warm glow of God's love.

5. He satisfies (verse 5a). Another great word (compared with rice dishes, where you are hungry again in an hour!).

Quote: 'He'll lift your tattered soul into his arms.' (From a song by Stuart Penny)

6. He renews (verse 5b). Here is an opportunity to talk of the work of the Holy Spirit, who works in us continually.

7. He puts right (verse 6). The evil done to us is transformed. We are enabled to live in a right way towards ourselves and others.

Ending: What a lot God does for us! Now you must encourage your hearers to respond, to come and receive what God promises.

Quote: 'Lord, I am not worthy to receive, but only say the word and I shall be healed.' (Anglican/Roman Catholic Eucharistic prayer)

63. Healing Service

WHEN: Healing service. Bereavement and memorial services. Dealing with any of life's problems.

AIM: To show how Jesus both cares for us and helps us in times of need. We take a 'non-healing' incident as an unusual yet positive approach to healing.

BIBLE READING: Mark 4:35–41.

OUTLINE:

Introduction: Was/is the expression 'It's not fair!' familiar in your family? Give an example (not too serious) of an unfair event in your childhood. Life sometimes doesn't seem fair. It was like that for the disciples one night.

Hardship is here:

> **Quote/Story:** Robert Browning begins his poem 'Easter Day' with the unexpected first line 'How very hard it is to be a Christian'.

It all seemed so unfair to the disciples. They had followed Jesus, worked through the day, done as they were asked (verse 35), even taking him with them (verse 36). The result? A near disaster (verse 37). Is Christianity hard? Yes.

Quote: 'The Christian life doesn't get easier as one gets older.' (Alan Redpath)

It's no insurance policy, or everyone would buy in. It is no cloud cuckoo land and there will be illness, loneliness, bereavement, the aches and pains of getting older, the hurts of sin and suffering. But, with all this:

Heaven is here: Look who's in the back of the boat (verse 38). He's in the storm.

Quote: 'The Saviour has tried for himself all the experiences through which he asks you to pass; and he would not ask you to pass through them unless he was sure that they were not too difficult for your feet, or too trying for your strength.' (F. B. Meyer, *The Present Tenses of the Blessed Life*)

Talk about Jesus' rejection at Nazareth, his tears at the grave of Lazarus, the loneliness of Gethsemane and the beatings and physical agony before the cross. But he is also the one who has brought heaven: the miracle of all miracles.

Quote: 'Once you have swallowed the incredible idea of God living in the world as a man, everything else is completely logical.' (Spoken by Mary Magdala in *The Davidson Affair*, Stuart Jackman)

Lead into verse 39, to realise:

Help is here: Jesus has the answer because he is the answer; as when Thomas asks 'How can we know the way?' and Jesus replies, 'I am the way' (John 14:5–6). He shares the storm and saves them from drowning: that's why the cross. The storms are mighty: he is Almighty. So,

Hope is here: The lovely question of verse 40 brings the calm, even without the disciples' understanding (verse 41). It echoes Psalm 103:13. We must trust. Will we?

> **Quote:** 'To all who are tossed by the waves, you are the calm of the harbour, you are the hope of the hopeful.' (Severus of Thrace – martyred AD 304)

Ending: The occasion will determine where this talk is going. You must have your conclusion in mind thoughout: are you heading for a 'laying on of hands' or similar prayer ministry? Or is this a talk of encouragement or consolation? The elements are there for these, but you need to work out which 'storms' you are addressing, so the Master can calm, love and save in whatever the situation. A time of quiet for private response would be good. But don't back away from specific prayer: the courage with the type of ending you go for must be with you.

64. Sports

WHEN: Sports event. General use.

WHO: Young people. Non-Christians.

AIM: To use a sporting theme to encourage people to become Christians.

HINT: Keep it light and 'sporty'. Although the sport referred to is football (soccer), the talk can be adapted. You will find it useful to refer to both goalkeepers and goal scorers to compare with what Jesus does.

VISUAL AID: A football, hockey ball or something similar.

HELPER: Got a Christian sportsperson to share their story? A Christian football player would be ideal.

KEY VERSE: 'It is time to seek the Lord, that he may come and rain salvation upon you' (Hosea 10:12).

BIBLE READING: If you need a Bible reading (doubtful), then Isaiah 55:6–11 is good. Or try Acts 16:25–31.

OUTLINE:

Introduction: Football has 'borrowed' a Christian word – 'saved'. In football, 'saved' means the ball being stopped from going into the wrong goal, so it can go into the right goal. Christianity has the same idea!

What are we saved from?

1. **From sin.** The great killer disease of the soul. God says we've got it.

   Quote: 'The question is not what men themselves believe concerning their sin, but what God's word says about it.' (John Bunyan, *The Life and Death of Mr Badman*)

2. **From self.** We can't stop doing wrong.

   Quote: 'Saved of what if not ourselves?' (Juan Carlos Ortiz)

3. **From hell.**

   Quote/Story: The singer Barry Maguire was asked in a radio interview, 'Is Christianity escapism?' He replied, 'True. The whole ship is sinking. Jesus is the lifeboat. Either we go down, or we sail on for ever.'

   'The wages of sin is death' (Romans 6:23). The ball's going the wrong way – let's kick it the other way:

What are we saved for?

1. **For heaven.**

Quotes: 'The greatest use of life is to spend it for something that will outlast it.' (Henry James)

'I go to prepare a place for you.' (Jesus, John 14:2)

2. For yourself.

Quote: 'The vast majority of men exist but do not live.' (Benjamin Disraeli)

John 10:9 is great here: Jesus gives real life.

Quote: 'When will you understand that you can't carry anything without him (Jesus), not even yourself?' (Michel Quoist)

3. For others. Matthew 28:19 – others need saving, too.

4. For Jesus. To love and follow him.

Who are we saved by? Hosea 10:12 – 'The Lord'. 'Come to me' (Matthew 11:28).

Quotes: 'This heavenly roller-coaster ride whose tickets are only available for those who cannot pay.' (Malcolm Muggeridge, *Jesus*)

'Saved by his precious blood.' (C. F. Alexander, from the hymn 'There is a Green Hill')

'Justified by his blood' (Romans 5:9). Speak of the cost paid by Jesus, our Captain, to save us.

Quote: 'Only the power that made the world can make a Christian.' (John Wesley)

We need the Holy Spirit to change our lives (1 Corinthians 12:3).

When are we saved? Now: 'It is time' (Hosea 10:12). 'Come now' (Isaiah 1:18). 'Call on him while he is near' (Isaiah 55:6).

How are we saved? 'He may come' (Hosea 10:12). You could use Isaiah 55:6–7.

Ending: Go for it! Invite your hearers to pray with you. Lead them in a simple prayer of trust, encouraging them to let you know they have done so at the end. Why should we settle for a ball being saved and not ourselves?

65. Sports

WHEN: Sports event.

WHO: Men. Young people.

AIM: To show that, whatever our condition, we can join the team of Jesus Christ, with him as our Captain.

HINT: Although Bible readings are given, you are very unlikely to read them when you speak, unless in a church service. Because of the use of the word 'captain', the KJV (Authorised Version) is good for the Hebrews reading, as it uses that word in verse 10.

BIBLE READINGS: 1 Samuel 22:1–4; Hebrews 2:5–10.

OUTLINE:

Introduction: Start on any topical sporting note about a successful team, especially one led by an inspirational captain or manager. Say how *you* are part of an amazing team, with a unique Captain. Say it with assurance: you are a Christian, Christ is your Captain. Tell your hearers that you have a great story to show who can be part of this team.

Explain how one or two people in the Bible are good illustrations of Jesus as Captain – David is one. Tell the story, briefly, of David's call to be leader, of Saul's opposition, getting to 1 Samuel 22:1. The people who joined him are the same people who join Jesus (all in verse 2).

In distress: Ask what distresses your hearers in our world today: war, famine, cruelty, sickness, environmental disasters, abused children, death – you get the idea.

> **Quote:** 'When you look at our scientific achievements and then look at our world today, what do we see? Crime, violent crime, increasing everywhere; pollution, noisome pollution, increasing everywhere; corruption, corroding corruption, increasing everywhere. When we see this, surely we recall the words of 2,000 years ago, "What does it profit a man, if he gains the whole world and loses his own soul?" ' (Lord Denning, when Master of the Rolls)

Ask if we don't need all the help we can get in this needy world: Jesus offers his help.

In debt: Say that David's team were not good people – nor are those who come to Jesus. Explain how we all have a debt of sin to God with all our wrong thoughts, words and deeds. But, amazing news: Jesus has died to wipe out the debt. Now we are:

> **Quote:** 'In debt to Christ.' (Douglas Webster, *In Debt to Christ*)

Discontented: Admit that none of us is completely satisfied with our lives.

Quote: 'Man lost his centre and so became eccentric.' (Bishop Festo Kivengere of Uganda)

Agree that some of us have no real idea why we are here on planet earth.

Quotes: 'We have nothing to live for. We have no aims any more.' (Sue Goy, social worker)

'I sometimes wake up at 8 o'clock in the morning wondering why I exist and why I'll die.' (Françoise Sagan, French writer)

Say how much we need a captain!

The Captain: Go back to 1 Samuel 22:2, where David became the 'leader' of these sorry people and gave them new purpose and hope. Jesus came:

Quote: 'To bring life back into living.' (Revd Roger Woodward)

Take your hearers to Hebrews 2:10 (AV), with Jesus as 'the captain of our salvation'. Talk of his triumphant life, rescuing death and glorious resurrection and how he now brings us courage to face the world, pays our debt and gives abundant, eternal life. Explain it means changing sides – a very costly step: Hebrews 13:13 is good.

Ending: Simply ask who will come over to the side of Jesus – a minority team which wins, with us giving all we've got.

66. Wedding

WHEN: Wedding. Marriage renewal service.

AIM: To encourage the couple to let Jesus be a key member of their marriage, relationship and lives.

HINTS: Compared with talk 67, this is much more for those who are part of the 'hatch, match and despatch' set, who rarely go to church but want a church wedding. They will probably only know 1 Corinthians 13 and choose that as 'the wedding reading'. Try to get them to agree to the short reading here, as an and/or.

You will need to know the story of Luke 24:13–35, although this is too long and inaccessible for the reading.

VISUAL AID: This talk relies on two cards (especially the second one) which give you your punch-line. Take two pieces of firm card, preferably A4, lightish in colour. Fold them in half to make A5 sizes. They will then look like blank orders of service/wedding invitations. On the front of the first, put ME. On the back put U +. On the front of the second one put US. Place this close to the fold. On the back put JES (coming up to the fold). Don't show the cards until the talk says so!

BIBLE READING: Ecclesiastes 4:9–12.

OUTLINE:

Introduction: Start with the inevitable 'Delighted to be asked . . .'. Then explain that life moves on and today is a big move for the happy couple. First comes:

ME: Show card one, front only. Being on your own is no great shakes.

> **Quote:** 'Ultimately he was a lonely person – we're all lonely.' (John Arlott, cricket commentator, speaking of the Welsh writer Dylan Thomas when interviewed by Michael Parkinson in 1971)

Say that God agrees: quote Genesis 2:18. Look at the bride as you say that the only thing 'not good' in the whole creation story was that man was alone: creation was perfected with woman! So now it is:

U + ME: Open up card one.

> **Quote:** 'When God created man, he created an individual. When God created woman, he created an entirely different thing: he created a society.' (John Dyer)

As you will not want a talk to non-churchgoers to be too 'heavy', you could use either of the following to say that today's union may give a man an occasional reason to question whether it is a good idea. . .

> **Jokes:** 'Marriage begins when you sink into her arms, and ends with your arms in the sink.'

> 'When a tree falls in the forest, and no one's there, does

it make a sound?' (Age-old philosophical question) Compared with: 'If I make a statement and my wife's not there, am I still wrong?' (Both from Andrew Platt, former Vicar of All Saints, Sudbury)

But today, U + ME has become **US**. Show the front of card two, ensuring the back is not exposed. Remind them of the reading: Ecclesiastes 4:9a. Your prayer is for the couple to be so happy that they will agree with this quote:

Quote: 'Although there will be no marrying, or giving in marriage, I hope that, when I get to heaven, I can live next door to my wife.' (Richard Hudson-Pope, children's evangelist, after his wife's death after over 50 years of marriage)

Now say how marriages these days don't seem to last. Are the words of this following quote true?

Quote: 'Nothing is so good it lasts eternally . . . no one in your life is with you constantly, no one is always on your side.' (Tim Rice, song 'I Know Him So Well' from the musical *Chess*)

You have great news . . . because US can include:

JESUS: Open the card! Tell the story, very briefly, of the two going to their home one Sunday, thinking Jesus was dead (this is the 'road to Emmaus' in Luke 24:13–35). You only need to make the wonderful point from Luke 24:15 that 'Jesus himself came up and walked along with them', and together they all went home.

Bring them back to Ecclesiastes 4:12, especially its ending: that's how the marriage can be secure.

Ending: Tell them 'Well done' for coming to God to bless their marriage and urge them to go on as they have started, with the presence of Jesus to bless them every day.

67. Wedding

WHEN: Wedding. Marriage renewal service. Short talk. Church anniversary. Baptism. Valentine's Day.

AIM: To bring God's blessing.

HINT: This is a very adaptable talk. The outline will concentrate on a wedding service, but it can be used in a great variety of situations, whenever a word of encouragement is needed. If this is a marriage renewal service, simply use the past as well as the present tense.

BIBLE READING: Numbers 6:22–27.

OUTLINE:

Introduction: After the 'What a joy to be here' bit, ask the couple what people have been saying to them. Suggest things like 'All the best' (how good is that?); 'Take care' (how?); 'Every happiness' (here's hoping); 'Good luck.'

Now say that you have one which is the oldest and the best. 'Good luck' could go back 3,000 years to the Psalms.

Quote: 'We wish you "good luck" in the name of the Lord.' (Psalm 129:8, in the Book of Common Prayer, 1662)

But yours is 1,000 years older: read out Numbers 6:22–27.

Simply walk through each section, without lingering too long on each.

'The Lord bless you and keep you': Say how all our good wishes are passing, but God not only wants to bless today, but to keep his blessing going. This marriage is God's gift. Turn to the groom with the following quote to show God's goodness to him:

> **Quote:** 'This letter is just to tell you that my mind is full of the greatness of God's gift to me when he put you at my side. Keep this thought of mine in your generous heart.' (Rodin, French sculptor, famous for *The Kiss*)

'The Lord make his face shine on you': If you are not using this talk for a wedding, but for another 'blessing' situation such as a church anniversary, you could have Philippians 2:1–11 as a second reading. In any event, Philippians 2:9–11 works well here: Jesus is the best and he gives his resurrection life blessing, shining on us (Revelation 1:16b).

'And be gracious to you': Tell the groom he's bound to get a few things wrong! No marriage can say, 'Never a cross word.' We should forgive each other and let God forgive us, too: that is why Jesus died. Sometimes we need more than love: explain how God gives us undeserved love – grace, hence 'gracious'. If we receive God's grace, all will be well.

> **Quote/Story:** When the wife of J. C. Ryle, the first Bishop of Liverpool, died, he had these words put on her tombstone (from 2 Kings 4:26, AV) ' "Is it well with you? Is it well with your husband?" She answered, "It is well." '

'The Lord turn his face towards you':

Quote: 'Here's looking at you, kid.' (Humphrey Bogart to Ingrid Bergman in the film *Casablanca*, 1942)

Story: A story from Selwyn Hughes tells of a small boy who holidays with his father. The boy is put to bed and the father goes for an evening meal. He later tiptoes into the dark room and gets into his adjoining bed. In the darkness, the boy whispers, 'Is your face towards me, Daddy?'

Explain how God is looking, with love, at the couple – and at everyone present. Ask if we are looking back.

'And give you peace': Yes, please! Say that we all want that, in our hearts, our homes, our relationships. It may not necessarily mean 'quiet'.

Joke: For the bride: 'When your husband snores, say to yourself, "He's alive. He's asleep. And he's in my bed!" ' (Carolyn Howarth)

Ending: Ask, 'How can all this happen?' The secret is in Numbers 6:27. The best illustration is a stamp on an envelope: the monarch's head gives it authority. God wants to stick with us. You could wrap the whole thing up by re-quoting the blessing, almost as a final prayer.

68. Young People

WHEN: School assembly.

WHO: Young people. Men.

AIM: To encourage young people (this will work, if slightly adapted, for men) to see that they can be key people in God's kingdom.

HINT: This talk should be given with lots of encouragement. It is based on God's call of Jeremiah: the verses are from Jeremiah 1 unless otherwise shown.

BIBLE READING: Jeremiah 1:4–12.

OUTLINE:

Introduction: Assuming your audience is made up of young people, say how there is nothing more boring than being continually asked, 'What are you going to do?' Say how the best answer is, 'I'm going to university to study business management with a view to going into industry', which really means 'I'm off to the South of France to soak up the rays and do nothing for the rest of my life, if only Dad would give me the necessary'!

Now say you have amazing news: God has something

hugely better in mind. Here is someone young, long ago, to whom God spoke: Jeremiah.

Hey – you! Say how we are talking about 665 BC, with the great King Josiah on the throne. Show that Jeremiah was very young (verse 6). Tell your hearers that their age is no problem to God: he wants to call them – personally.

> **Quote:** 'The heart of religion lies in its personal pronouns.' (Martin Luther)

Use verse 4 ('to me') and link it with the personal calls to Moses (Exodus 3:4), Gideon (Judges 6:12), Samuel (1 Samuel 3:10), Paul (Acts 9:4), and any others which are your own favourites. God knows, and calls, your hearers – however young.

Say how wonderful this is: we are personally loved. Use Revelation 3:20, John 6:37 or John 3:16 to give personal assurance.

> **Quote:** 'Every promise of God is made to me.' (Martin Luther)

Who, me? Try and make Jeremiah's objections come to life with some animation: can't speak, too young (verse 6). Go on to show how others reacted similarly: Moses (Exodus 3:11; 4:10), Isaiah (Isaiah 6:5), Peter (Luke 5:8).

> **Quote:** 'God has an exasperating habit of laying His hands on the wrong man.' (Joe Blinco)

Say how we all feel inadequate. But. . .

This is the way: Where will God's call take your hearers? Three answers:

1. **Where to go.** 'Go to everyone I send you to' (verse 7). You could draw on John 14:6 and Proverbs 3:6. Tell your hearers to have a big view of the possibilities God has for them.

   Quote: 'Give me Scotland, or I die.' (John Knox, as he paced his garden)

2. **How to speak.** 'Say whatever I command you' (verse 7). Tell your hearers it was a command to Jeremiah – and it is to us (Romans 10:9–10).

   Quote: 'We cannot keep silent about the good news we have been given.' (Roy Williamson, former Bishop of Bradford)

   Explain how the world desperately needs the good news of Jesus: will we give it?

3. **How to have power.** Go to the great promises in verses 8 and 18. We can't – but God can.

   Quote: 'Without God, we cannot. Without us, he will not.' (Augustine)

   Will there be opposition? Yes (verse 17). Will there be victory? Yes (verse 19). God gives us his power and his words (verse 9).

Ending: Ask your hearers: who dares? God calls them: who will go for God? Say how Jeremiah went for God all his life.

Quote: 'Most people are made by the times. Some people are made for the times.' (R. T. Kendall)

TIMES OF HARDSHIP AND ENCOURAGEMENT

69. Winning

WHEN: Hard times. Men's meetings. Ladies' meetings.

WHO: Leaders. Sports people. Men. Ladies.

AIM: To show, from a great Old Testament incident, that we can know God's victory in the difficult situations we face in our individual lives, our churches and our country.

HINT: It would be wise to check the previous two or three chapters before the Bible reading and to bring the reading in where suggested.

BIBLE READING: 2 Chronicles 20:1–12.

OUTLINE:

Opening quote: 'To me, there's only one thing in life, and that's success.' (Kevin Keegan, England soccer manager, after victory against Hungary put England into the World Cup Finals, November 1981)

We all want to be winners. But we face:

The opposition:

– **In the world.** Pollution, pornography, war, famine:

pick the ones you want to mention, referring to Ephesians 2:2 and the power of evil.

- **In the church.** Divisions, fear to share the faith, concerns about offending others, especially other religions:

   Quote: 'The crisis of the church today is not primarily doctrinal or moral. Above all we face a crisis of powerlessness.' (David Watson, *Be Filled with the Spirit* booklet)

- **In ourselves.** Romans 7:15 is strong stuff, especially from a Christian leader.

The problem: 'We don't know what to do.' We are not the first to say this: someone beat us to it.

Tell the story leading up to the reading: the land of Israel has divided. Only two tribes are in the south, with Jehoshaphat as King of Judah. Three huge nations have besieged them in the city of Samaria, threatening to exterminate them.

Now read the Bible reading, 2 Chronicles 20:1–12.

Show how, for them, the enemy was too powerful. For us too, repeat that our lives get in a mess, along with our churches and our world.

The answer: It would work well simply to read verse 12. The story does not end until verse 30 and verse 13 is delightfully poignant, especially the picture of the 'little ones'. In their need they cry out to God. Admit that you say 'I don't know what to do', but that you forget the rest of Jehoshaphat's words, which are the secret to success.

The victory: You will need to tell the unfolding story with drama and enthusiasm: how God told the people he would win for them (verses 15–17); how the people did as they were told and how delighted they were (verses 22–23).

Explain how God intervened for us, too, through the amazing life, death and resurrection of Jesus: in his life he never sinned, his death paid for sin and the resurrection brought proof of victory and everlasting life.

> **Quote:** 'The evil world will not win at last because it failed to win the only time it ever could.' (P. T. Forsyth)

This is a victory the church needs to rediscover.

> **Quote:** 'The early Christians did not say in dismay, "Look what the world has come to!" but in delight, "Look what has come to the world!" They saw, not merely that sin did abound, but that "grace did much more abound".' (Dr Stanley Jones)

A good Bible quote is 1 Corinthians 15:57.

What must we do?

1. Trust. As well as verse 12, verse 17a is good here: no point running, the enemy was too fast; no point fighting, the enemy was too strong. Stand: say how we should stand to be forgiven and receive God's life and power.

> **Quote:** 'If our hearts were only in living dependence upon God our experience would be one of continual victory.' (Henry Groves)

2. Go. But only with God: verse 17b. Then we can praise

(verse 22) and enjoy: verse 25 is great – speak of God's wonderful blessings to us.

Ending: The key verse, 12b, can be a lovely prayer. Invite your hearers to quietly bring whatever is their greatest concern and say those words as a prayer.

70. Confidence in God

WHEN: Hard times.

WHO: Older people. New Christians.

AIM: To encourage Christians to face their problems head on and see that they can trust God to get them through.

BIBLE READING: Psalm 11.

OUTLINE:

Introduction: You could go straight in with, 'Do we want to be Christians – even when the going gets tough?' Say that the safe way may not be the best way, or even the right way. Our old friend King David will give us some clues, five of them, each starting with 'Tr'.

1. Trouble. Verse 2: a man in crisis.

Quote: 'Houston, we've had a problem.' (Call from the spacecraft *Apollo 13*, April 1970)

Show how, for Christians in some countries, the opposition is intense (verse 3). But, in your experience, trouble comes more subtly, the enemy will 'shoot from the shadows' (verse 2). We never know when problems will come, or how. But sometimes things get very tough.

2. Trickery. The temptation is to run away: draw from the end of verse 1. Say how we may be given well-meaning but wrong advice, as when Jesus said he had to go to die and Peter said, 'Don't', bringing the 'Get behind me, Satan' from Jesus (Matthew 16:21–23). This is where you refer to verse 3, saying how our problems can feel overwhelming. If you are older, you could say how temptation seems to get even more subtle and strong. How important to have a strong faith:

Quote: 'Woe to the man who has to learn principles at a time of crisis.' (Ray Steadman)

You may want to paraphrase what follows, because of its dated language, but it is a strong comment on Psalm 11:

Quote: 'Are we tempted to put our light under a bushel, to conceal our religion from our neighbours? Is it suggested to us that there are ways of avoiding the cross, and shunning the reproach of Christ? Let us not hearken to the voice of the charmer, but seek an increase of faith, that we may wrestle with principalities and powers, and follow the Lord, fully going without the camp, bearing his reproach. Mammon, the flesh and the devil will all whisper in our ear, "Flee as a bird to your mountain"! But let us come forth and defy them all. "Resist the devil and he will flee from you." There is no room for retreat. Advance!' (C. H. Spurgeon, *Selections from the Treasury of David*)

3. Triumph. Point to verse 4, showing that God is not running away. Compare with verse 3 – his foundations are not being destroyed. Jesus is our great high priest in the temple (Hebrews 4:14). God is for us (verse 7): so we win.

4. Trial. Admit that we rarely hear a preacher speak on the theme of verses 4b–6, but there is judgement. It is not a popular concept today.

Quote: 'Wrongdoing is met by an advertising campaign, but never by a word of judgement.' (David Bubbers)

Agree with verse 6 – it is true. But, right now, we can escape from the trial:

Quote: 'The judge is also the Saviour.' (David Jenkins, former Bishop of Durham)

Which brings you to the last 'Tr':

5. Trust. Share the loveliness of verse 7, and that God loves us as we trust him.

Quote: 'No one is more trustworthy than the God of the cross.' (John Stott, *The Cross of Christ*)

Ending: Go back to the opening words of the psalm, encouraging your hearers to turn them into a prayer.

71. God Cares

WHEN: Hard times.

WHO: Christians. Non-Christians. Parents. Prisoners.

AIM: To show God's love and care for us, by taking two of the three occasions when Jesus raised someone from the dead, to demonstrate his heart of compassion.

EXPLANATION: This is an unusual talk, being based on two completely separate incidents which are invariably viewed singly. However, by linking them you will be able to show unique aspects in the approach of Jesus to them – and to us.

BIBLE READINGS: Luke 7:11–17; John 11:17–44.

OUTLINE:

Introduction: Open with a smile and a comment along the lines of, 'I don't know about you, but sometimes I need all the help I can get!' Say how friends rally round, family is good, but what you really need is God's help: hence today's readings. The bringing back from the dead of the young man in Nain and Lazarus at Bethany can speak to us all.

The help of the Saviour: Draw from the fact that the impetus, in both incidents, was with Jesus: 'Jesus went' (Luke 7:11); 'Let us go . . . Jesus came' (John 11:15, 17). Jesus knows where the trouble is: he comes to calm our fears.

> **Quote:** 'Fear is so common to us that the words "Fear not" come in the Scriptures no less than 366 times – one for every day of the year, including [a] leap year!' (David Watson, *Be Filled with the Spirit* booklet)

You could make a couple of extra points:

1. Jesus goes to just one widow (Luke 7:12): his help is for the individual.
2. In each case, his disciples go along with him (Luke 17:11; John 11:16). You can ask your hearers if we are there, with Jesus, to help those who need him – and us.

The hope of the Saviour: Go to Martha's sad comment in John 11:21 and the response of Jesus (verses 25–26).

> **Quote:** 'Stay your faith upon Christ; not upon your most hallowed feelings, but upon Christ himself and his written promises. Whenever you are in doubt, perplexed, or unhappy, go at once to the Lord and his unfailing word, and God's truth will disperse any mists of darkness which surround your soul.' (Dr R. E. Speer)

Show how God has a higher perspective than we do and can bring his hope to see us through whatever we face. 'The stone' (John 11:39) can be removed: whatever prevents help getting through to our need.

Quote: 'Christ alone can turn suffering into satisfaction, our tests into testimonies, our trials into triumphs, and our pain into peace: if we'll let him.' (Billy Graham)

The heart of the Saviour: Make a big thing of the way Jesus cares in these two incidents. Luke 7:13 – 'His heart went out to her'; John 11:33, 35, 38 – 'He was deeply moved . . . and troubled . . . Jesus wept . . . Once more [he was] deeply moved'.

Quote: 'Jesus, with his gentle judgement and severe mercy.' (Simon Barrington-Ward, former Bishop of Coventry)

Show how he brought the answers because he really cared, was fully involved, even to weeping.

Quote: 'Intensity of grief is related to the degree of involvement, not just to love.' (Peter Morris)

It would be particularly good to bring your hearers to the ultimate heart of Jesus for them – on the cross, using Isaiah 53:4. He has entered our human tragedies as no other has.

Quote: 'The other gods were strong, but thou wast weak;
They rode, but thou didst stumble to a throne.
But to our wounds only God's wounds can speak,
And not a god has wounds, but thou alone.'
(Edward Shillito)

Ending: Ask your hearers if they will let Jesus come to them to help them with his hope and his heart of love. A time of quiet would not be inappropriate, with an offer for prayer ministry.

72. Don't Worry

WHEN: Hard times.

AIM: To encourage your hearers not to worry (as we all do), but to trust in the Saviour who loves them.

EXPLANATION: All verses quoted are from the reading, unless otherwise shown.

BIBLE READING: Luke 12:22–34.

OUTLINE:

Introduction: Ask your hearers if they ever worry. Say how we would all rather be happy. The secret?

> **Quote:** 'Trust and obey, for there's no other way
> To be happy in Jesus, but to trust and obey.'
> (J. H. Sammis, from the hymn 'When We Walk
> with the Lord')

Let's see how Jesus said we should do it:

Don't worry about life: Set the reading in context: it follows the story of the rich fool, who had everything and yet nothing. The disciples' problem was the opposite – had they given up too much? In our materialistic society, say how important this is for us 'disciples' (verse 22). Talk about how our culture is possession-mad and then quote verses 22 and 23. Show how Jesus takes his disciples to the birds and their dependence on God: he wants a similar trust from us.

Verse 27 is lovely too, about God's care, with verse 25 showing how useless worry is, whichever translation is correct (one has length of life, the other making ourselves taller).

Don't worry about food: Point out that verses 29 and 30 are not saying 'Don't work well' or 'Don't provide', but that God knows about all our needs. Ask if we really believe this and, even if we do, do we live in its truth? Now ask: what should we care about?

Care for the kingdom of God: Show the secret in verse 31.

> **Quote:** 'Family, work, even church activities, cannot be allowed to diminish God's primacy in our lives.' (Walter Brovald)

Is God's kingdom our concern? Take your hearers back just one chapter, to the Lord's Prayer: 'Your kingdom come' (11:2). Be sure to show the amazing result, at the end of verse 31, if we do.

> **Quote:** 'Obedience to his will today means that God assumes the responsibility for our tomorrow.' (Charles Allen)

Care for true riches: You could give the comment about how much people leave when they die, the answer always being 'everything'. How do your hearers feel about verse 33?

Quote: 'There is this feeling in you that you are a stranger, that this is not your habitat. You're here. It's rather nice, rather interesting, no criticism of it, particularly. But it is not where you belong. You are a displaced person.' (Malcolm Muggeridge, interviewed in *The Daily Telegraph*, August 1975)

Show how this motivates us to care for others (verse 33a). We may not need to sell up: Peter had a home (Mark 1:29), as did John (John 19:27) and Mary and Martha (John 11:20). But we need to be able to say:

Quote: 'This world is not my home
I'm just a passing through.'
(From a song by Albert E. Brumley)

Ending: As you draw all these thoughts to a conclusion, here is a lovely prayer with which you could end:

Quote: 'Father, help me to entrust the past to your mercy, the present to your love and the future to your wisdom.' (Frank Colquhoun)

73. The Great Provider

WHEN: Hard times. Church anniversary.

WHO: Church leaders. Christians.

AIM: This is a talk to encourage entire congregations rather than individuals. It is especially appropriate at times of difficulty or opportunity, or at a major milestone in a church's life.

EXPLANATION: This is based almost entirely on the reading – the verses are from there (unless stated). Be encouraging as you give it, lifting your congregation.

BIBLE READING: Revelation 3:7–13.

OUTLINE:

Introduction: It is a corny line, but you could begin by telling your congregation that you have brought them a great bunch of sweet peas to encourage them. All your points are great and all begin with 'P'! But first, a quick setting of the scene: the reading was about a church in a city founded in Turkey in the second century BC by the King of Pergamum. His brother, Attalus, had been so loyal he had earned the name Philadelphus. The church there is also

loyal – to Jesus. He writes to them personally – as he does
to us here today. A 'P' for each verse:

1. **A great Potential** (verse 8). Show how the Philadel-
   phia church is not strong and how we, as a church, often
   feel that way. But God is giving that church an 'open
   door' of opportunity – and us, too. No one can stop this –
   quote the verse. Ask if we are willing to go on with God.

2. **A great Power** (verse 9). Speak of God's power being
   so much greater than ours, and how this little church
   (and ours) has victory assured.

   Quote: 'We can serve, not because we have the power,
   but because we have the right connections.' (Alan Bod-
   dington)

   You could link the end of verse 9 with 1 John 4:4, showing God's love combining with his power.

3. **A great Pat-on-the-back** (verse 10). Admit that this
   heading is fairly dodgy in your 'Ps'! But it says what the
   verse does: God congratulates the Philadelphians for
   being faithful – and he wants to encourage us similarly.

   Quote: 'When we get the victory within we can face a
   thousand worlds.' (R. T. Kendall)

   Show how they needed this encouragement, bearing in
   mind the second half of the verse. Ask your hearers if
   they are ready for some difficult times and if they realise
   that God will see them through. Go on in Revelation to
   12:11 to show how the victory is won now and into the
   future. This will lead you naturally to:

4. A great Promise (verse 11). Announce the good news – Jesus is coming! Ask if we have this hope, or are we, unlike previous generations, forgetful of this final victory?

Quote/Fact: Charles Wesley wrote 7,270 hymns. Of these, 5,000 were to do with the second coming of Jesus.

Say how we want to give Jesus glory on that day – with our church's crown ready for him.

5. A great Palace (verse 12). Simply read the verse, enthusing about this ultimate destination. Emphasise that entry is dependent on our individually belonging to Jesus as our Saviour, not our being members of this church.

Quote: 'The pathway to heaven does not consist in following a set of rules but loving a person. It is not guaranteed by belonging to an outward body or organisation, but by committal to one who saves and keeps.' (Eric McLellan, former Vicar of the Embassy Church, Paris)

6. A great Possibility (verse 13). The last verse is for us, tell your church. Will we hear?

Ending: Ask if we will go forward with Jesus. He can do it.

Quote/Story: The soldiers of Alexander the Great told him they were vastly outnumbered. He asked them, 'How many do you count me for?' as they went out to win. We have a far greater leader.

74. The Eternal Optimist

WHEN: Times of encouragement.

AIM: To encourage Christians to accept themselves and their value to God: to turn them from pessimism to optimism.

HINT: This is a talk which relies heavily on both readings. You could bring in the John reading at the beginning of the second point.

BIBLE READINGS: Romans 8:12–17; John 10:7–15.

OUTLINE:

Introduction: Start with something along the lines of, 'I've got a "pick-me-up" for all of us today, so we can go out feeling optimistic!' You could use this quote:

> **Quote:** 'There has been created a prejudice in favour of doubt over faith. The phrases "blind faith" and "honest doubt" have become the most common of currency. Both faith and doubt can be honest or blind, but one does not hear of "blind doubt" or "honest faith".' (Lesslie Newbigin, *Proper Confidence*)

Ask if your hearers are optimists or pessimists as you begin with:

A touch of realism: Bring your talk to the Romans reading, acknowledging that we all have a 'sinful nature' (verse 12), echoing Romans 3:23.

> **Quote/Story:** In the story 'The Eye of Apollo', a man sets up a new religion. The detective Father Brown has a companion who speaks of this: ' "It claims, of course, that it can cure all physical diseases." "Can it cure the one spiritual disease?" asked Father Brown, with serious curiosity. "And what is the one spiritual disease?" "Oh, thinking one is quite well," said Father Brown.' (G. K. Chesterton, *The Innocence of Father Brown*)

If you have used both readings already, the first half of John 10:10 fits here, as does Romans 8:13a. This is realism.

> **Quote:** 'I was much too far out all my life,
> And not waving but drowning.'
> (Stevie Smith, poem 'Not waving but drowning')

The reason for optimism: Bring your hearers to the John reading, especially verse 11, and show how Jesus has died for us – the greatest rescue act of history. To be clever, say how the Greek emphasises his uniqueness: 'I am **the** shepherd, **the** good and excellent one', emphasising the word 'the'.

Take them back to verse 9 and ask if they are in or out. The optimists are on the inside!

Optimism for ever: Start with the John reading, showing that we have to be optimists when we see what we are and have as Christians:

– 'Saved' (verse 9): a lovely safe word.

- Fed: talk about the 'pasture' (verse 9).
- Abundant life: enthuse about the greatness of the words in verse 10.

Now move to the Romans reading for four more:

- Led by God's Spirit (verse 14).

   Quote: 'It is God's love and grace that sets our inner conflicts and chaos in order. It is his Spirit who remakes us at the heart of our being.' (*The Times*, editorial, Christmas Eve, 1998)

- 'Sons of God' (verse 14). Rejoice with your hearers in such a title: we are not slaves; we have the 'spirit of sonship' (verse 15).
- Intimacy with God: 'Abba, Father . . . God's children' (verse 15). Here is a remarkable fact for your hearers: God is referred to as 'Father' only 11 times in the whole of the Old Testament. Jesus addresses him as 'Father' 170 times in the Gospels (over 100 in John), telling his followers to use that word (Matthew 6:9).
- 'Heirs of God' (verse 17): all that is God's is ours – including suffering.

Optimist or pessimist? Tell your hearers that you have told them the truth, but we often live as if we did not believe it.

   Quote: 'People can dare to trust God.' (David Jenkins, former Bishop of Durham)

Ending: Close along these lines: If you've got it, live it, believe it, enjoy it, share it. Let's go home optimists!

BEING CHRISTIANS

75. It's for You

WHEN: Pentecost.

WHO: New Christians. Non-Christians. Seekers.

AIM: To help Christians and non-Christians alike to see that Christianity really is for them personally. God is for us.

HINT: This is another of those talks which is quite expository in that it relies primarily on unlocking the passage: the verses are from the reading, unless stated.

BIBLE READING: Ephesians 3.

OUTLINE:
Introduction: Say how great it feels to be the bringer of good news, so you are feeling particularly pleased with a talk full of excellent news. Ask your hearers if they realise how special they are, because God is for them and Christianity is for them, as you will now demonstrate. Your hearers are to do three 'Fs':

Be Favoured: You could use the old adage that 'familiarity breeds contempt' to say how we have lost the wonder of verse 6: we Gentiles are now an 'in' people. 'Everyone' (verse 9) is favoured, Jew and non-Jew alike. The cross of Jesus has worked the wonder (verses 11–12). We are special!

Quote/Story: Johann Tauler of Strasbourg met a peasant. 'God give you a good day, my friend,' he said. The peasant answered, 'I thank God I never have a bad day.' Tauler, astonished, said, 'God give you a happy life, my friend,' with the reply, 'I thank God I am never unhappy.' 'What do you mean?' asked Tauler. 'When it is fine, I thank God. When it rains, I thank God. When I have plenty, I thank God. When I am hungry, I thank God. And, since God's will is my will, and whatever pleases him pleases me, why should I say that I am unhappy when I am not?' 'Who are you?' 'I am a king.' 'A king? Where is your kingdom?' The peasant replied, 'In my heart.'

Show Paul's reaction to his being a favourite in verses 8 and 9, going to others with the great news. Ask if we do.

Be Family: We are part of the family of humanity (verses 14–15). Ask if your hearers allow God to be part of their homes and families, giving their family the dignity God intended for them.

Quote/Story: Carl Jung, the Swiss psychiatrist, was asked if he believed in God. He replied, 'I don't believe; I know.' On the lintel of his home in Küsnacht, he had carved, *'Vocatus atque non vocatus deus aderit'* – 'Called or not called, God will be present'.

Ask whether your hearers let God be part of their family and also if they are truly part of the family of the church, which is verses 18 to 19a. Say how, in the original Greek, the words 'with all the saints' are emphatic – no opting out (Hebrews 10:25 helps here). We share God's love with others corporately (verse 10).

Be Filled: Share that God wants to fill our lives:

– **All of him.** Draw from verses 16, 17 and 19 to show the triune 'Spirit', 'Christ', 'God' doing this: strength, faith, fullness.

Quote: 'It is no good giving me a play like *Hamlet* or *King Lear*, and telling me to write a play like that. Shakespeare could do it; I can't. And it's no good showing me a life like Jesus and telling me to live a life like that. Jesus could do it; I can't. But if the genius of Shakespeare could come and live in me, I could write plays like that. And if the Spirit of Jesus could come and live in me, I could have a life like that.' (Archbishop William Temple, quoted by David Watson in *My God is Real*)

– **For all of you.** 'The inner being' (verse 16); 'hearts' (verse 17). Say how God wants to be central: Lord.
– **With all he's got.** Go to verse 16 and on to the splendour of verses 17 to 19. Say them with passion and wonder, showing how God wants to bring the very best from him to us.
– **Through all his power.** Here are verses 20 and 21: say that God can do it.

Ending: Smile as you say you make no apologies for your enthusiasm: the last 'F' is yours; say it with 'Feeling'. People stood to pray, unless they were deeply moved: verse

14 is Paul's – and yours. What you've shared really matters – do your hearers agree?

> **Quote:** 'The keys to effective evangelism are wet eyes, bent knees and a broken heart.' (Stephen Olford)

76. Good Friends and Fellow Workers

WHEN: Family service.

WHO: Christians. Children. Ladies.

AIM: To show how we need each other and, especially, Jesus.

HINT: This could be quite a fun talk, with a lot of interaction with your hearers; which is why it would work well with children, or with children present. Try for as much audience participation as possible.

BIBLE READING: Philippians 2:19–30.

OUTLINE:
Introduction: Ask if there's anyone your hearers don't like in the church – but they mustn't call out names!

   Quote: 'To dwell there above,
              With the saints that we love,
              That will be glory.
              To dwell here below
              With the saints that we know–
              That's another story!'
              (Henry Brandt, psychologist)

Now say that we'd rather talk about people we do like. So, let's find out who is:

My best friend: Ask: who? And: why? Have yours ready – perhaps your partner. Try to avoid the answer 'Jesus', because he comes later. (Probably the best way to avoid this is to say, 'If your best friend is Jesus, give me your second best friend!') This is meant to be light-hearted. Wander round if you can. Ask who was Paul's: you could have Colossians 4:14 as one idea (Paul was often ill and needed a friendly doctor).

My most helpful friend: Do it again – who? And why? Have you got one (a DIY genius, for example)?

Now bring in the first half of your reading, explaining how helpful Timothy was to Paul (verses 19–24). Timothy helped Paul – and Jesus, too.

> **Quote/Story:** The Venerable Bede writes about Bishop Cuthbert and a priest called Herbert: 'They inspired each other with intoxicating draughts of the life of heaven.' (From *Ecclesiastical History of the English People*)

Ask if we have someone we are helpful to, or are we not helpful at all?

> **Quote:** 'See how these Christians scratch one another.' (Tony Baker, former Vicar of Christ Church, Cheltenham)

My bravest friend: Again: who? And: why? You might know someone bravely facing illness, an operation, even death or bereavement. Bring in the second half of the reading, talking about Epaphroditus nearly dying, but still going on to help Paul and serve Jesus. You could draw on others who have been brave Christians.

Quote/Story: Margaret Wilson was 18 when she and her older friend, Margaret Lachlison, were accused of being Christians in the seventeenth century in Scotland. They were tied to stakes to drown as the incoming tide rose, the older woman nearer the sea. Margaret Wilson was asked what she thought of her friend. 'What do I see but Christ wrestling there? Do you think that we are the sufferers? No, it is Christ in us.' Both drowned.

The best friend: Say you are offering no prizes for this one: yes, it is Jesus! Proverbs 18:24 is lovely: show how Jesus is the 'friend who sticks. . .'. Hebrews 13:5 comes in well, too.

Quote: 'God is, he is as he is in Jesus, so he is for us.' (David Jenkins, former Bishop of Durham)

You could comment on how Peter says we can bring all our hurts and problems to him, using 1 Peter 5:7. He is, then, the best and most helpful friend. Say how he is the bravest, too, as he died for us.

Quote/Story: The famous theologian Karl Barth visited the University of Chicago. After his lecture, a student asked: 'You know more of the Bible than we ever will. What is the greatest thing you have discovered?' He replied, 'Jesus loves me, this I know, for the Bible tells me so.'

Ending: Simply encourage your hearers to value their friends, to be good friends and, especially, to enjoy the friendship of Jesus.

77. The Good Guys!

WHEN: Christian meetings.

WHO: Christians. Men. Leaders.

AIM: To encourage Christians to be the best – loving, caring, forgiving, playing as a team.

HINT: This is a really positive talk about some of the best qualities found in Christians, so you can be up-beat throughout, urging your hearers to live such lives. All the verses (bar one) come from the reading.

BIBLE READING: Philemon (all of it!).

OUTLINE:

Introduction: Ask your hearers what sort of people they would really like to be: kindly, generous, good friends, caring – the good guys? You have news for them: such people do exist and we can join them. Joke how you will need a whole book of the Bible to prove it, but it only has 25 verses!

You could give a short background, explaining how Paul knew Philemon well, and how Philemon's slave Onesimus has run away, met Paul in prison, become a Christian and is now returning home. The reading could come here.

Give further details about the heroes of the book:

Philemon: A good guy: Go through the different ways Philemon shows his love:

1. **He loves Christian work.** You could use the Amplified translation of verse 1: 'Philemon, our dearly loved sharer with us in our work'. Ask your hearers if they are team players in the work of the church.

   Quote: 'One hand cannot clap.' (Jamaican proverb)

2. **He is loved by Paul.** The Good News Bible in verse 9 has 'I love you'. Point out that the world cannot understand Christian love, but it is real – draw from 'brother' (verse 7), 'grace . . . and peace' (verse 3) and 'grace . . . with your spirit' (verse 25), coupled with Paul's prayers (verse 4) to show his heart-love.

   Quote: 'Love is supreme and comes before service; even before soul-winning. God is love, and the more we grow like Jesus the more love we shall show towards others.' (Major Allister Smith)

   Show how Paul wishes Philemon 'every blessing' (GNB verse 6): ask if we are similarly generous.

3. **He loves God's people.** Quote from verses 5 and 7. If you are using the KJV, avoid 'The bowels of the saints are refreshed by thee' (verse 7)! Rather, use the NEB: 'I am delighted and encouraged by your love'. Ask if we are generous here, too.

4. **He loves God.** You will want to point to this being the big one (verse 5). Say how we start here.

Onesimus: Good guy number two:

Quote/Story: A humble Christian entered a very aristocratic church in a strange place. 'Do I know you?' asked the usher. 'Do you know Jesus Christ?' the man replied. 'Yes.' 'Well, I'm a poor relation of his.'

Make something of Paul's play on words: 'Onesimus' means 'profitable' – hence verse 11. Now he is a Christian, Jesus has made him good: and verse 16 is true, which leads to Paul's request (verse 17).

Quote: 'A community of acceptance.' (Julian Charley, speaking about the church)

Ask your hearers if they welcome new folk, and if they have changed lives.

Paul: Good guy number three: Share, from verses 17 to 19, what a generous, positive encourager Paul is, speaking so humbly, even though he is so great. Do we go the 'second mile'?

The team: All the good guys: Don't forget verses 23–24: the hard-working crew, all 'fellow-workers'.

Quote: 'Christians are members, not of a club, but of a crew. They are not in church to sit around and be waited on. They are there to fulfil specific functions.' (Eddie Gibbs)

Give a quiet word of warning: check 2 Timothy 4:10 to see what happened to Demas.

Ending: Simply say to your hearers: let's do it; let's be like these fine Christians in our church today.

78. Teamwork

WHEN: Christian meetings.

WHO: Churches. Fellowships.

AIM: To encourage your hearers to be part of their church or fellowship in an active and positive way, as members of 'the body of Christ'.

HINTS: This talk would be particularly appropriate if a church/fellowship has plans for moving forward and needs encouragement to do so. It would also work if there were signs of division or discontent. In any event, it is a good idea to preach this sort of talk from time to time to inspire togetherness among Christians.

BIBLE READING: Ephesians 4 (long, but good).

OUTLINE:
Introduction: This depends on the state of play when and where you are speaking. You need either (a) 'Isn't church great!' (b) 'Wouldn't it be good if we could get it together as a church?' or (c) 'I really love being part of this church!' Then say how the reading was the blueprint for how a church should be: we're a team. We should do three things:

Play as a team: Quote verse 3 and say that, more than any other letter, Ephesians deals with spiritual battles, even in heavenly places. You could refer to 3:10 and 6:12, pointing out that the devil has a team. We will win if we stand together (verse 4).

> **Quotes:** 'By uniting we stand, by dividing we fall.' (John Dickinson, *The Liberty Soup*)
>
> 'The church is not a religious movement, it is the corporate Christ.' (Alan Nute)

Speak of the cruel, hostile, divided world, and compare it with how we are to be in verse 2, emphasising the 'every effort' from verse 3: it's not easy. Say how we do not listen to verse 26 and fall out too easily, being like silly children, compared with verse 15. If only verse 32 might become increasingly true of us!

> **Quote:** 'God doesn't want individual potatoes, he wants mashed potatoes, "that they may be one".' (Juan Carlos Ortiz)

Play as a team member: Say that each of us has a part to play, with our varied gifts from God (verse 7): emphasise the word 'grace' – God's undeserved love (acrostic: God's Riches At Christ's Expense). We need each other.

> **Quote:** 'Wherever my Lord has a true believer, I have a brother.' (Bishop McIlvaine)

Show how this applies especially to leaders, using verse 11. There cannot be one leader who does everything. Give the reason from verse 12 – so all will be blessed and built up, going to the word 'all' in verse 13, with the diversity of gifts giving corporate unity. If your hearers will not play their individual parts, the team is weakened and the aim thwarted. Ask them: 'What's your part?' And ask if they encourage the leaders.

> **Quote:** 'To make Christianity a solitary religion is to destroy it.' (John Wesley)

Play under the Captain: Use verses 4 to 6 to show how we are to be a team under the triune leadership of Father, Son and Holy Spirit. Speak of any team needing leadership: our answer is in verses 15 and 16.

> **Quote:** ' "Where two or three are gathered together in my name, there am I" is not 1+1+1=4, but 1+1+1=1.' (Graham Pulkingham)

You could be very clever and say how the Greek for 'joined together' in verse 16 is *harmos*, a body word meaning 'shoulder joint', keeping the body illustration. Compare 'humble' in verse 2 with Jesus in Philippians 2:8: he can show us how to do it. We need this help.

Ending: Enthuse your hearers to be like that. You could ask them where we need to change to have a church/fellowship along these lines. Why don't we talk about it after the service?

79. New

WHEN: General use.

WHO: New Christians. Church leaders. Non-Christians.

AIM: To enthuse new Christians to live new lives with Jesus; to get church leaders to lead their churches forward; and to encourage non-Christians to come into a new way of living.

BIBLE READING: Luke 6:1–16.

OUTLINE:

Introduction: Whenever we read of incidents in the Bible, they are part of a wider picture. The context of Luke 6 is that it follows chapter 5 (obviously), where Jesus has been talking about his kingdom being like new wine. Now he will show what this means in three ways. Things will be different from now on.

> **Quote:** *The Taste of New Wine.* (Title of a book by Keith Miller)

New Master: 'Jesus Christ is Lord' (Philippians 2:11). See also John 13:13. Here in Luke 6:1–5 we see how he is to be Lord over the way we live.

Quote: 'There is not a square inch of life about which Jesus Christ does not say, "It is mine." ' (J. Kneiper)

The example given is of behaviour on the Sabbath. The extra-scriptural rules of the Pharisees are overturned, because of verse 5. The NEB uses the word 'sovereign'. It would be good to point out that Jesus changes a negative 'can't' to a positive 'can'. So often Christianity is perceived today as 'Thou shalt not': not according to Jesus.

Quote: 'The way of obedience is not to make your own work plan and ask for the Lord's signature, but to ask for his plans and write your signature.' (Corrie ten Boom)

New motivation: Verses 6 to 11 bring another Sabbath confrontation, with another negative becoming positively new. It moves us on from showing that Jesus is Lord to why that is so: to bring a new attitude to life and to people.

Dr Luke has a medical attention to detail, even to which hand is the problem (verse 6). Should Jesus follow the religious custom, or care for the man?

Quote: 'Jesus Christ did not come to bring us a religion, he came to bring us a life.' (Juan Carlos Ortiz)

Jesus cares: this is our motivation, too. People may not understand: you could draw out the reaction in verse 11. It is tragic because the Pharisees could have received a new outlook on life. Do we let Jesus give us the motivation of his care and love?

New men: This is an all-inclusive word, although because of the times the disciples were all men. Verses 12 to 16 show his new team.

Quote: 'He spent all night thinking things out in prayer.' (Alan Dale's paraphrase of verse 12)

You may want to mention this care through prayer before talking about the twelve. They were the raw material of the kingdom and were a very unusual selection (you could give a couple of examples). They needed training, strengthening, helping and welding into a team. But Jesus calls them to make them new.

Quote: 'They gave themselves away to Christ that day, without any reserve, and following Jesus means no less than that today. In spirit it is essentially the same abandonment of life to him. That is where much of our modern Christianity falls short: we do not bring enough of ourselves to him, we do not commit ourselves to him and his way of living.' (Ridley Chesterton)

Don't forget to strike the cautionary note that Judas of Kerioth (Iscariot) was included: a mere 'office' does not save. We have to let ourselves be made new when Jesus calls us.

Ending: Revelation 21:5 is true of heaven – and of the kingdom now. We have a new Lord with a new reason for living. We are to be new men and women.

Quote: *Live a New Life.* (Title of a book by David Watson)

80. The Teacher

WHEN: Christian meetings.

AIM: To show how vital the teaching of Jesus is for our Christian lives, and how we need to be both close to him and obedient to what he says.

EXPLANATION: This talk takes an unusual approach to the Beatitudes, because it looks at Jesus himself and his hearers, rather than at the Beatitudes themselves (with which we can become over-familiar).

BIBLE READING: Matthew 5:1–12.

OUTLINE:
Introduction: You might want to tell your hearers not to panic – this is not yet another talk on the Beatitudes. You have a new angle, looking at the bit before the teaching.

Only those who should were there: As you are majoring on verses 1 and 2, you could simply quote them, emphasising that it was Jesus' choice to 'go up' above the crowds, and how it was only the disciples who shared the climb. This enables you to make the point that much of Jesus' teaching is for those who belong to him.

Draw on the new relationship Christians have with God through Jesus: you could use Matthew 6:9. It is a new life and a new lifestyle.

Quote: 'You say I never sing about anyone but Jesus, well that's because Jesus is my song.' (Anne Herring, lead singer of Second Chapter of Acts, from 'Jimmy's Song')

Say how we need to learn privately, with a passing reference to Mark 4:10. This does not exclude others: Matthew 4:23–25; 7:28; 8:1–2. But there are times for us and Jesus only.

Only those who would might share: 'His disciples came to him' (verse 1). Speak of their volunteering and paying the price of climbing. Not all will agree with this next quote:

Quote: 'Life is only for love. Time is only that we may find God.' (St Bernard)

Ask if we are making the sacrifice to come apart to learn of Jesus. Are we genuinely seeking to know Jesus and his will for our lives?

Quote: 'Hunger for God is the genuine mark of a disciple.' (George Verwer, *Come, Live, Die*)

You could explain that there is even a difference between those who want Jesus as Saviour and those who also know him as Lord of all they are and do. There is to be a seriousness of learning, and also in living:

Quote: 'The word "Saviour" is used two dozen times in the Bible; the word "Lord" is used over 600 times in the New Testament.' (Juan Carlos Ortiz)

Only those who could will dare: Now (at last) you can bring your hearers, briefly, to the Beatitudes themselves. Say what a tremendous challenge they are: who lives like that? It is all but impossible.

Show how Jesus did not pat his disciples on the head with a 'well done for coming'. Compare this with many of our cosy, comforting Christian messages. Pick out two or three from verses 3 to 12 to show that they are not only uncompromising messages, but alien to our modern culture. Maybe they always were!

> **Quote:** 'God hath called you to Christ's side, and the wind is now in Christ's face in this land; and seeing ye are with him, ye cannot expect the lee side or the sunny side of the brae.' (Samuel Rutherford, 1600–61)

Point to the radical changes Jesus expects from his teachings. Who dares?

Ending: The Teacher brings a new life and lifestyle. Will we climb the hill to let these be ours?

> **Quote:** 'The important thing is this: to be able at any moment to sacrifice what we are for what we could become.' (Charles du Bois)

81. Potential!

WHEN: Baptism. Pentecost.

WHO: New Christians. Young People. Seekers.

AIM: To show how God has plans for our lives, whoever we are.

HINT: The talk is based on the choosing of young David to be king. It is an excellent story, so bring it to life.

BIBLE READING: 1 Samuel 16:1–13.

OUTLINE:

Quote: 'I went to the woods today because I wanted to live life deliberately – to suck the marrow out of life. So that, when I get to the end of my life, I don't find out that I've never really lived.' (Robin Williams, in the film *Dead Poets Society*)

Introduction: After using this quote, set the scene (check 1 Samuel 15 for this). Tell the story, very briefly, of the first king of Israel, Saul, failing, and how God wants 'a man after his own heart' (1 Samuel 13:14). He has someone in mind.
Explain that there are some big lessons here for us today.

Man's standards are not God's standards: Build a glowing picture of Eliab, Jesse's eldest son: big, strong, good-looking soldier – Samuel was convinced (verse 6). Then bring in the impressive words of verse 7 – God's stunning response. You could use Isaiah 55:8 here. Eliab was going his way, not God's.

> **Quote:** 'One time I went to a man and asked him to come and join the church and give his heart to God. He responded, "I can't do it." "Why?" I asked. "Well, I have my reasons." "My friend," said I, "will you go home now and write a reason which you think will satisfy God if you were called to him at this moment?" The next day he came to me, deeply affected and said, "I can't find a reason that would do up there – not one." ' (Sam Jones, 1898).

You might want to use Romans 3:23 here, or, even better, Jeremiah 17:9–10. That's the negative. But:

Man's potential is known to God: Dramatically take your hearers down the line of Jesse's sons (verses 8–10), with their failure, to the crazy question of verse 11 and its sad reply: David was a nobody, not even in the line. 'Only a boy' (1 Samuel 17:42). Now show what God says: 'This is the man' (verse 12b, NEB).

> **Quote:** 'Boys will be men.' (Richard Hudson-Pope, altering the proverb, 'Boys will be boys'.)

Speak of God seeing the potential in young David – the one who wrote Psalm 8:4–5.

> **Quote:** 'It's not how many seeds are in the apple, but how many apples are in the seed.' (Graham Penny)

Say how David could have been a life-long shepherd. God had bigger plans. Ask your hearers if they believe Revelation 1:5–6, making us very special people: do we believe God can and will do great things with us?

> **Quote:** 'Some believe that God is Almighty and can do all; and that he is All-Wisdom and may do all; but that he is All-Love and will do all – there we stop short.' (Julian of Norwich)

Ask if we are in danger of not realising our potential, of not finding true satisfaction.

> **Quote:** 'He spent his life searching for a satisfaction, in his work and private life, which he never seemed to find.' (Ex-wife Britt Ekland about Peter Sellers, just after he died)

Man needs God's Spirit to realise his potential: Come to verse 13, showing the secret of David's success. God makes all the difference – especially if we get things wrong: David's prayer in Psalm 51:10 fits here. Speak of how the Spirit can come on your hearers: will they let this happen?

> **Quote:** 'A question of willingness.' (O. Hallesby, *Why I Am a Christian*)

Ending: Explain that most of us will not end up as kings and queens – but we can achieve our potential with God's help. Who among your hearers will let God 'anoint' them?

STIRRING THE SAINTS

82. Who's in Charge?

WHEN: Youth groups and gatherings.

WHO: Young people. Christians.

AIM: To encourage Christians to be 100 per cent for Jesus Christ.

KEY VERSE: Romans 6:16.

BIBLE READINGS: Romans 6:9–23. Also John 8:31–36 and Galatians 5:16–25.

OUTLINE:

Introduction: It could be a good starter to say that Paul, one of the greatest church leaders ever, sometimes spoke of himself as a 'servant' of Jesus Christ, the word originally meaning a 'bondservant' – a willing slave. That's how he introduces himself in Romans 1:1. He is asking his readers whose servants they are: a question to us, too.

Here are four facts:

Fact 1: Someone is in charge: A good contrast is in Galatians 5:16–25, where Paul writes of the 'desires of the flesh' and the 'fruit of the Spirit'. We are on one side or the other: Matthew 6:24 is helpful.

Quote: 'I believe in free will; but then it is only a will to act according to nature. The sinner in his sinful nature could never have a will according to God. For this he must be born again.' (J. Denham-Smith, *The Gospel in Hosea*)

The question is, who is in charge of you? If your hearers (especially at a youth event, when someone calls out 'I am!') say they are, or think they are, they need first to hear. . .

Fact 2: The evil one can be in charge: John 8:34 is one of the Bible's key verses. The first sections of Romans 6:16 fit here. This is the state of everyone (unless the next fact is true), as Romans 3:10 and 23 point out.

Too often we 'flirt' with sin: this may be literally true, as 2 Corinthians 6:14 shows. If we think we are in charge, why do we keep doing wrong? Why are we not getting our lives right?

Fact 3: Jesus Christ can be in charge: Here is the second part of Romans 6:16, and the brilliant answer to John 8:34 in John 8:36.

Quote: 'Children, I commend you from the bottom of my heart into the captivity of the cross of our Lord Jesus Christ, that it may be in you, over you, behind you and before you, lying heavy on you and yet received by you with free and full acquiescence to the will of God, whatever it may please him to do with you.' (Anon, fourteenth century)

Make sure you put this fact across positively: compare the

two halves of Romans 6:11. Also, 2 Corinthians 5:14–15 is good: the RSV has it translated, 'The love of Christ controls us'. We are set free from sin to accept freely a new form of being slaves: Romans 6:18.

Quote/Story: John Livingston was a seventeenth-century Scottish Covenanter. He wanted to be a doctor, but God called him to be a preacher. He said, 'From then, I had one passion and it was he, he alone.' (Quoted by Alexander Smellie in *Men of the Covenant*)

Fact 4: We need to ask Christ to be in charge:

Quote: 'If we are to enter into, and continue in, God's way for us, we must not have plans of our own. Two people cannot control one life. God has his way for you. If you have a way for yourself, then it is not under control and cannot be until you surrender your programme and accept his.' (Dr W. Graham Scroggie)

Ending: The last bit of Romans 6:19 is good, as is the amazing contrast in Romans 6:23.

Quote/Story: Alexander the Great gave away all his possessions before setting out to conquer the world (which, eventually, he did). His best friend asked him, 'What have you kept?' Alexander replied, 'Hope, and a vision of a great kingdom.' His friend responded, 'Then take back the village you have given me and let me share that hope.'

We are called to God's kingdom: let's give all we have for it.

83. Who Dares Wins

WHEN: Sports event.

WHO: Men. Young people. Church leaders.

AIM: To throw out a big challenge to your hearers to stand out as God's people. It will be particularly appropriate for men, and works well with young people, who will rise to a dare.

HINTS: This is not a talk for faint-hearted speakers! You need the nerve to go for it. If you do, you will be amazed at the positive way your hearers respond. If you use the reading (it's a good one), practise beforehand – there are some big words!

BIBLE READING: 2 Samuel 23:8–17.

OUTLINE: 'I'm not going to give you a talk – I'm going to give you a dare!' would be a bold opening. Say how the world is in a big mess and needs people to stand up and be counted. We have lots of men in sport, politics, business and so on – but where are God's men? God's mighty men even? You will introduce three of them.

The marks of mighty men:

1. **They win victories.** Quote verse 8 (if you can!). The secret is at the end of verse 12. Say that most people, even Christians, make little, if any, difference. But God's mighty men do.

   Quote: 'On graduation day, God will bestow on you the degree of DD – devil destroyer.' (Agrippa Khathide of Cape Town)

   You should quote further from 1 Corinthians 15:57. We are to go and beat evil, winning many for God's kingdom.

2. **When others quit, they stand firm, until the work is done and the victory is won.** Use verses 9 and 10, with a reference to 1 Peter 5:10. Paint the picture with a flourish – the taunts, the sword frozen, the victory. Do the same with verses 11 and 12, including the farmer's displeasure at losing his lentils! The first bit of Colossians 1:23 is good. Who dares to hang on in with God?

3. **They go at great cost.** The crazy request of David in verses 13–17 saw the mighty men risk their lives. We hardly ease out of our armchairs!

   Quote: 'It must cost you not less than everything to follow Jesus.' (Simon Barrington-Ward, former Bishop of Coventry)

4. **They do it for love** (verses 16b–17).

   Quote: 'If Jesus be God, and died for me, then no sacrifice can be too great for me to make for him.' (C.T. Studd)

It is true – Jesus has given his all for us: where is our loving response?

5. They lead others. A glance at 1 Chronicles 27:2, 5 and 8 will show that each of these men led 24,000 others. Mighty men encourage many to go for Jesus.

The making of mighty men: Here is the great hope for every one of your hearers: go back to 1 Samuel 22:2 to see where the mighty men began – as ordinary, needy nobodies. Only the great leadership of David led them to trust in God, through whom they won. We need Jesus to be our leader, to bring us to God and his Holy Spirit's victory.

Quote: 'We have to be grace-motivated.' (David Bubbers)

Bring your hearers to the cross of Jesus for his forgiveness and to his resurrection for his power. That is where mighty men are made.

The maybe of mighty men:

Quotes: 'Who dares wins.' (Motto of the British Special Air Service (SAS) regiment, from 1942)

'If you commit yourself to the love of Christ, then that is how you run the straight race.' (Eric Liddell, Scottish athlete and missionary, as spoken in the film *Chariots of Fire*)

Ending: Now you need your courage to call your hearers to be God's mighty men. Let MM stand for mighty men, not Mickey Mouse . . . and dare to dare!

84. The Glory of Life

WHEN: Youth groups. Men's meetings. Ladies' meetings.

AIM: To enthuse people to put God first in all they are, have and do.

HINT: This is a very tough talk, with many challenges to your hearers. Be brave, speak about your own struggles: a 'holier-than-thou' style would be disastrous.

> **Quote:** 'We're all learners here.' (George Green)

BIBLE READING: If you need one, Matthew 6:25–33 would work. However, the talk is a walk through Jeremiah 9:23–24, which is too short for a reading.

OUTLINE:

Introduction: Why not go for a head-on opening along the lines of, 'I'm going to tell you the whole truth: Christianity is a revolution of life and lifestyle. Here are a couple of verses from the Bible to give you the idea.' Then quote Jeremiah 9:23–24. If you are talking to church people, here's another:

> **Quote:** 'Someone warns us lest we become so heavenly-minded that we are of no earthly use. Brother, this

generation of believers is not, by and large, suffering
from such a complex! The brutal, soul-shaking truth is
that we are so earthly-minded we are of no heavenly
use.' (Leonard Ravenhill, *Why Revival Tarries*)

Is your glory in yourself?

Quote: 'I did it my way.' (Paul Anka, writing for Frank
Sinatra)

1. **Wisdom.** Your nerve will determine the questions you
pose about whether God controls the way we think.
What about what we watch on TV, our attitude to science
and creation, the way we vote, our approach to the Bible,
our studies, our 'intellectual' arguments? 'Let not the
wise man boast of his wisdom' (verse 23) sits well with
Proverbs 3:7, 1 Corinthians 1:25 and 1 Corinthians 1:19
(quoting Isaiah 29:14). Say how you struggle with the
challenge of Romans 12:2.

2. **Strength.** This may be even tougher if your audience is
men: what about our bodies being under God's control?
You could mention the way we behave with sex, the way
we drive, play and watch sport (do we get more worked
up about our favourite team than about God?).

Quote: 'I have conquered an empire, but I have not
been able to conquer myself.' (Peter the Great, Czar of
Russia)

'Let not the strong man boast in his strength' compares
with God's 'weakness' in 1 Corinthians 1:25.

3. Riches. Here's a hot potato! Are we too busy, or too lazy? Ask about how we earn our money. Is shopping a god? Do we always need bigger, better and more expensive? The story of Luke 12:13–21 is serious, especially the last verses. Check what riches can do in Mark 4:19.

Quote: 'What a tragedy to climb the ladder of success, only to discover that the ladder was leaning against the wrong wall.' (Erwin Lutzer)

Is your glory in God? You could use 1 John 2:15–17, or the essence of it.

Quote: 'At 41, I was at the pinnacle of power; I had everything I could dream of. Yet I was empty inside. A strange hollowness within me persisted, even in the midst of wealth, success and power.' (Charles Colson, senior aide to President Nixon in the Watergate era)

State that, for the Christian, 'Your God will be your glory' (Isaiah 60:19). Psalm 3:3 is good, too. Take the first half of Jeremiah 9:24, linking it with 1 Corinthians 10:31. Now take the positives of understanding and knowing God from Jeremiah 9:24:

1. 'Steadfast love', also translated 'kindness'. Say that anyone can be an unkind bully. Where are the generous, kind and caring? This takes real strength and can only be done with the love of Jesus.

2. 'Justice'. Ask if we are active in society to promote good, with no snobbishness or prejudice.

Quote: 'It is necessary only for the good man to do nothing for evil to triumph.' (Allegedly Edmund Burke, but not traceable in his works)

3. 'Righteousness'. Say this means, simply, to live right!

Ending: Take your hearers to Jesus, who always pleased his Father: John 8:29 is amazing. Do we live otherwise? Or do we want God to be pleased with us? The ending of Jeremiah 9:24 anticipates Jesus. Ask who will let God fill them with his power to be that sort of person.

85. Life Among the Believers

WHEN: Communion/Eucharist.

WHO: Church members. Church leaders.

AIM: To look at the life of the first-ever church, see how they did things and ask if our church today works along these lines.

HINT: There is a wealth of material here. If you feel one or two points need special emphasis for your particular situation, skim over the others. In any event, beware of talking too long on one point and not having time for the rest.

BIBLE READING: Acts 2:37–47.

OUTLINE:
Introduction: An opening question could be, 'How do you think we should "do" church these days?' Agree that this is a burning topical issue. Now suggest that it might be an idea to go back to the beginning, to see if we can get a few tips from the first-ever church. First, we must be:

In: Show how most people started outside: verse 37. No doubt they were 'good' and 'religious', but they needed to follow verse 38. They were not the last:

Quote: 'I went perhaps farther than many of you do; I used to fast twice a week, I used to pray sometimes nine times a day, I used to receive the sacrament constantly every Lord's day; and yet I knew nothing of Jesus Christ in my heart.' (George Whitefield)

Point to the good news in verse 41: lots came in. Then they could go. . .

On: This is where you walk through verses 42 to 47. (Don't tell your hearers you have 13 points – it would be very off-putting: only mention it at the end!) How did the church set out to be church?

1. 'Devoted to teaching' (verse 42). Ask if your hearers are really enthusiastic about hearing God's word taught.
2. Fellowship (verse 42). Speak of the importance of us being in Christian friendship together.
3. They broke bread (verse 42). Do we share in the bread and wine, whatever we call the service? Explain how this has been a key element in Christianity from the beginning, fulfilling Jesus' command (Luke 22:19).
4. Prayer (verse 42). Show how vital this was as they grew.

   Quote: 'Wherever throughout the world I have traced a spiritual awakening to its cause and centre it has always been found in a prayer life that was beyond the ordinary.' (Dr J. R. Mott)

5. They were 'filled with awe' (verse 43). Be honest – this is not noticeable in most congregations: ask if we have lost, or forgotten, this one.

6. Miracles and wonders (verse 43). Ask if we have missed out here, too. Do we believe in these today? Ask your hearers: if not – why not?

7. 'Everything in common' (verse 44). Ask: how is our caring and sharing for and with each other?

8. Helping each other's needs (verse 45). This takes the previous point even further: ask if we go as far as to sell our possessions to help our poorer brothers and sisters. Probably not!

9. Meeting in God's house – every day (verse 46). Show how they knew they needed God, not just each other.

   Quote: 'The church is not a self-help group.' (Lindsay Urwin, Bishop of Horsham)

10. Lots of hospitality (verse 46). Encourage this!

11. They were 'glad' (verse 46). Ask if we are happy!

    Quote: 'Happiness, by definition, means "a good god within" – from the Greek *"eudaimonia"*.' (Marcus Aurelius, AD 121–180, *Meditations*)

12. 'Sincere' (verse 46). Do we really mean what we're doing?

13. 'Praising God' (verse 47). Hooray, you can say, at last here is one we do!

You could ask how many we got out of the 13.

Out: Two points here, from verse 47: everyone outside was pleased the Christians lived like this, and every day (imagine that) more became Christians.

Ending: You could say, 'Wow!' Ask if your hearers would

like to be a church as good as that and then ask if it isn't time we made a start. Suggest we talk this through together, and make a few positive changes.

SONGS OF PRAISE

86. Amazing Grace

WHEN: Songs of Praise event. Evangelistic event. 'Tricky Questions' session.

AIM: To use either the hymn 'Amazing Grace' or the song 'Only by Grace' or similar to speak of how we become Christians.

HINT: Any song about us being saved through grace alone will work: the above two would work well. The reading is key to this; the verses are from there unless otherwise indicated.

BIBLE READING: Luke 13:22–30.

OUTLINE:

Introduction: You could get right into the talk without preliminaries by saying that we all have 'hot potato' questions for God – and we are not the first to do so. When Jesus was on his tours, people were for ever asking tricky questions – our reading had one: 'Are only a few people going to be saved?' And the answer? Let's answer with a few other questions:

How are we saved? Start with Jesus' own answer: verse 24a. You could put this in the context of Luke 13:3 and 34, with their warning and love. We have to admit our need to repent.

> **Quote:** 'If we don't admit we are sick we shall never go to a doctor. Jesus can help us when we admit our sinfulness. We all know in our hearts that we do sinful things. The good news is that when we confess our sins humbly to Jesus he forgives us and makes us clean. Whatever our sin, we should not think it too bad to be forgiven. We come to Jesus today in repentance.' (Vincent Nichols, RC Archbishop of Birmingham, *Walk With Me – Christmas Readings 2001*)

Then you could go to Ephesians 2:8–9 and use your hymn or song, drawing out the need for God's grace, not our efforts.

> **Quotes:** 'Amazing grace, how sweet the sound.' (John Newton, hymn)
>
> 'Only by grace can we enter.' (Gerrit Gustafson, song)

Bring out the fact that it is only through Jesus that we receive a new life, being 'saved' (verse 23). Matthew 7:14 fits here, too.

> **Quote:** 'What is this new life? It is a new relationship with God.' (Colin Scott, Bishop of Hulme)

Are there few? Only those who respond.

When are we saved? Show from verses 24–27 that the implied answer is 'Now'. One day it will be too late (verse 25).

> **Quote:** 'When the door into the Kingdom is eventually shut – and we should notice the solemn fact that one day

it will be shut – there will be many shut out who thought they were going in.' (David Gooding, *According to Luke*)

What if we are not saved? Speak of the serious words in verses 27 and 28 – words of the loving Saviour Jesus himself. Verse 30 shows many 'first' ending 'last'.

What if we are saved? The second half of verse 28 plus verse 29 is worth enthusing about.

Quote: 'They shall sit down with Abraham, Isaac and Jacob and rest for ever from warfare and work.' (Bishop J. C. Ryle, *Expository Thoughts on the Gospels – Luke*)

Accentuate the positive: it is wonderful to be saved!

Ending: You could refer back to Luke 8:8b: we need to hear and respond – the 'narrow door' (verse 24) is open. We can be saved by Jesus today.

Quote/Story: The comedian Spike Milligan was asked, 'Of all the people who have ever lived, who would you most like to meet and take out to dinner?' He replied, 'Jesus Christ.' 'Why?' 'Because I'd just like to meet him.' (From *An Audience with Spike Milligan*, ITV, February 1996)

87. 'Salvation Belongs to Our God'

WHEN: Songs of Praise event. Worship service.

WHO: Non-Christians.

AIM: To speak of the wonder of God's salvation.

HINT: This talk can be used with any hymn or song which refers to 'salvation', not just the one suggested by the heading. It is based on the reading – the verses are from there, unless otherwise shown.

BIBLE READING: Isaiah 12.

OUTLINE:

Introduction: As this talk is likely to be used at a worship service of some sort, you will have chosen the song/hymn to follow, so a good way in is to say, 'I've chosen a favourite song for us to sing in a few minutes' and tell your hearers what it is. Here are a couple:

> **Quotes:** 'Salvation Belongs to Our God' (Adrian Howard and Pat Turner, song)
>
> 'Visit us with Thy salvation.' (Charles Wesley, from the hymn 'Love Divine')

If you use this style, or not, you could ask if your hearers ever get really excited: a beautiful view, passionate love, a sporting victory? Bring them to your reading – a man excited over something wonderful: quote verses 1 and 2.

Show how he stumbles over his words, using 'the Lord' twice (verse 2). Talk about the salvation Isaiah describes, especially the forgiveness in verse 1. Bring in the way God made this happen through Jesus' death on the cross. Draw out the three-fold meaning of 'salvation' from those first two verses: 'comfort', 'strength', 'song'. Be excited yourself about these and how positive they are.

Now come to the three things we have to do to respond to this 'salvation'. We are to:

Get it: Verse 2: 'I will trust and not be afraid.'

Quote: 'To be reborn to a life that is ever new and full of hope, we don't need to go back to our mother's womb: we need to be "born from above", by opening ourselves up to the gift of the Spirit, for "what is born of human nature is human; what is born of the Spirit is spirit" (John 3:6).' (Pontifical Council for the Laity, 1999)

Say how easy it is to know this in our heads, or to try to get salvation our own way: point to verse 2, with its straight-forward 'trust'.

Quote: 'Ask people what they must do to get to heaven and most reply, "Be good." Jesus' stories contradict that answer. All we must do is cry, "Help!" ' (Philip Yancey, *What's So Amazing About Grace?*)

Grasp it: Now move to verse 3 to show how 'salvation' is not just a one-off but an ongoing experience and how we must let God continually fill us from his 'wells'.

> **Quote:** 'Faith is the empty hand which we hold out to God and which he fills with himself.' (John Calvin)

Do you have a story of blocking a water pipe or hose or standing on a spring of water, staunching the flow and then releasing it so the water came again? Say how we can block God's Spirit as Christians. Explain how, whatever our denominational background, we really need God's Spirit.

> **Quote:** 'God wants to fill me with his Spirit. I have been greatly misled if I see being filled with the Spirit as an optional extra in my life. It is for all who follow Christ. The Spirit is not reserved for any particular denomination or for any special types of Christian people.' (Colin Day, *I Believe*)

Enthuse about us being filled every day – grasping this 'salvation'. Thirdly:

Give it: Here come verses 4 to 6, telling others of God's 'salvation'. Ask if we are doing this, or keeping it to ourselves.

> **Quote:** 'Some want to live within the sound
> Of church or chapel bell.
> I want to run a rescue shop
> Within a yard of hell.'
> (C. T. Studd)

Ending: A prayer of response should lead into your song or hymn.

88. 'The Old Rugged Cross'

WHEN: Songs of Praise event with hymn 'The Old Rugged Cross' before or after the talk. Lent (when explaining the cross). Good Friday.

WHO: Older people (who remember this old hymn).

AIM: To show the balance between the 'good' and 'bad' bits of the Bible, between judgement and mercy. To explain the centrality of the cross.

BIBLE READINGS: Malachi 3:16 – 4:6; John 3:31–36. The verses which follow are from the Malachi passage, unless shown otherwise.

OUTLINE:
Introduction: Explain how preaching is a bit like walking a tightrope. The Bible gives two sides of one picture and you worry about giving one side without the other. This is a bad news/good news situation.

The two sides:

– **The bad side** (verse 1). This is not the Old Testament having a final hard fling before the good news of the New Testament. Show how the magnificent chapter of God's love (John 3) ends in a very dramatic way: John 3:36 (second half of the verse). And what about the shocking Hebrews 12:29? Who can say they never do 'evil' (verse 1)? Bad news indeed!

Quote: 'Every rejection carries a health warning.' (Keith Sutton, former Bishop of Lichfield, in 1990)

– **The good side** (verse 2). Look at the warmth, the healing, the new life. It's wonderful!

Quote: 'The Lord addresses personally "you who fear my name". Like calves released from their stall into the sunlight they will leap about with sheer relief and exuberance that right has triumphed.' (Joyce Baldwin, in her commentary on verse 2: *Tyndale Old Testament Commentaries: Haggai, Zechariah, Malachi*)

Show how God wants to warm our cold hearts with his love (1 John 4:10). He comes to heal our hurts, pain and sorrow with his touch, to breathe life into our dead souls.

The problem: How can you preach without being threatening and offensive on the one hand or too sugary and soft on the other?

The answer: It's in 'the old rugged cross', which speaks of both the bad and the good.

– **The bad is answered at the cross.** Show how sin is dealt with and paid for on the cross. Our judgement is taken by Jesus. The empty cross and tomb bring victory.
– **The good is answered at the cross.** This is no soppy,

sentimental love. This love is the greatest – strong, powerful and deep.

Quote: 'Upon the cross of Jesus
Mine eyes at times can see
The very dying form of one
Who suffered there for me.'
(Elizabeth Clephane)

Ending: We must let go of hell and all that holds us to it: the rich young ruler could not (Mark 10:22). We must let all heaven come, whatever the cost.

Quote: 'We want the Christ of the cross, but we don't want the cross of the Christ.' (Billy Graham)

There is no tightrope really: we are on one side or the other. Thank God for 'the old rugged cross'.

A final thought: If you can never speak like this and you never mention hell, consider this:

Quote: 'Once heaven and hell are completely deleted from the sermon, the church will have been culturally domesticated. God must at last surrender to human artifice, for then he will not be found either in the sermon or at the altar.' (Calvin Miller, *Marketplace Preaching*)

89. 'Shine, Jesus, Shine'

WHEN: Songs of Praise event. Preparation for evangelism. Easter season. Festival of Lights. Candlemas.

AIM: To enthuse about how great the Christian life is, thus encouraging others to enjoy living as Christians.

HINTS: The talk would work well with the Graham Kendrick hymn 'Shine, Jesus, Shine', or a similar hymn or song in a worship/Songs of Praise setting. If used in preparation for evangelism, show how the points help us to present the Christian message very positively. It walks through the reading: verses are from the reading, unless otherwise shown.

BIBLE READING: Psalm 36:5–9.

OUTLINE:
Introduction: Go for something like: 'Christianity is not meant to be a set of rules to follow – it's a life to live!' Be upbeat from the start. Say that you want to show this from a great bit of a psalm: read Psalm 36:5–9 with passion!

The love of life: Your aim here is to pick out the elements which show God's love in giving us his life. Draw from these:

– So great (first half of verse 5): the biggest love there is.
– So certain (rest of verse 5): God does not desert those he loves.
– So good (verse 6).
– So measureless (first bit of verse 7).

Speak of the amazing love we have from God both to enjoy and to offer to others. You could bring in Jesus' death, forgiveness, heaven – enthuse, but don't dwell too long – there's more! Ask if we live with this love.

> **Quote:** 'There are only two ways to live your life. One is as though nothing is a miracle. The other is as though everything is a miracle.' (Abraham Lincoln, quoted in the letter fronting *Saga Magazine*, June 2006)

The length of life: Use the rest of verse 7, plus verse 8, to show the value of a life which knows God: no favourites ('high and low'), a 'refuge' in hurting times, a 'feast' for our spiritual impoverishment, a 'river of delights' for ongoing blessing, flowing for ever. Throughout our lives we can know this.

> **Quote/Story:** When very old, a USA president was asked how he was: 'Thank you. John Quincey Adams is very well in himself, sir, but the house in which he lives is falling to pieces. Time and seasons have nearly destroyed it. The roof is well worn, the walls shattered. It trembles with every gale. I think John Quincey Adams will soon have to move out. But he himself is very well.' (Quoted by J. Oswald Sanders in *Enjoying Your Best Years*)

The Lord of life: Use the first half of verse 9 to show that only God can give this life.

> **Quote/Story:** When asked, 'How would you start a new religion?' Voltaire replied, 'You should arrange to have yourself crucified, and raised again on the third day.'

Mention the cleansing fountain from the blood of Jesus (1 John 1:7) and the fountain of the Holy Spirit (John 7:37–39).

The light of life: This is verse 9, part two. You could use the first part of 1 John 1:7 here. Jesus comes to bring light: hence Graham Kendrick's 'Shine, Jesus, Shine'. John 8:12 fits here, too.

> **Quote:** 'For if the Christian faith's untrue,
> What is the point of me and you?'
> (John Betjeman, from his poem 'Septuagesima')

Ending: If you are encouraging your hearers to go out to share their faith, tell them to take these words to others, with this advice:

> **Quote:** 'Do it simply. Do it well. Do it now.' (Matt Busby, Manchester United manager, to his 'Busby Babes' before they went to play a match)

Finally, sing 'Shine, Jesus, Shine' or a similar hymn/song.

FAITH-SHARING – BY US

90. The Life of a Christian

WHEN: Encouraging faith-sharing.

AIM: To encourage Christians to live positive Christian lives wherever they go and whoever they meet.

VISUAL AID: If you have the nerve, take some of your spray perfume (male/female) which has a pleasant but strong smell. Only spray it on very willing volunteers – you don't want to be accused of assault!

BIBLE READING: 2 Corinthians 2:14–17.

OUTLINE:
Introduction: Say how, in the old days, Christians were likened to an army – probably because of the wars being fought in the world.

> **Quote:** 'Onward, Christian soldiers,
> Marching as to war.'
> (Sabine Baring-Gould, hymn)

Admit that this may not be an appropriate picture today, but that Paul occasionally drew on military illustrations to prove his point, as we shall see today. What is the life of a Christian?

Winning: a life of triumph: The first half of verse 14 should help you to explain how the Roman army would capture enemy soldiers and parade them through their cities on returning from a campaign. Draw the contrast for us: Jesus has 'captured' us from the devil and now sets us free to be in his victory procession.

There are so many verses you could use here: pick a favourite or two from Philippians 4:13, Acts 1:8, Ephesians 6:13, Revelation 7:14, Revelation 12:11 and 1 Corinthians 15:57.

> **Quote:** 'When I'm gone, don't wonder where I'll be:
> Just say that I trusted in God and that Christ was in me.'
> (Bob Dylan, song 'Aint No Man Righteous')

Witnessing: a life of testimony: As you take the rest of verse 14, now is your chance to give a couple of people a spray – if they let you. Explain how everyone will know they have got your perfume/aftershave on: they smell of you! That's how we all are to be with Jesus: Acts 1:8, Matthew 5:16. The original, from which Paul draws, is of the incense wafted by the priests in the triumphal procession: soldiers and captives alike walked through the smoke and took its aroma away with them afterwards.

> **Quote:** 'Evangelism is the primary task of the church.'
> (Lambeth Resolution, 1988)

There are two sorts of 'smell':

1. **The smell of death.** Pick the relevant words from verses 15 and 16 which are negative. Admit that some will react negatively, as in 1 Corinthians 1:23. Enemy

towns hated the Roman army procession and the smell of incense. Show how Jesus had this happen to him (Luke 19:14) and warned us, too (Luke 6:26).

2. **The smell of life.** Here are the positives in verses 15 and 16: the Roman cities loved the incense. So we have 'good tidings' (Luke 2:10). We bring God's love to others.

Quote: 'The way from God to a human heart is through a human heart.' (Samuel Gordon)

Working: a life of commission: Ask your hearers if they noticed Paul's momentary hesitation in that great reading: the very end of verse 16. Even he has his personal doubts (e.g. Romans 7:24). Show how he realises he is 'commissioned by God' (verse 17, RSV) – like an army officer. The Great Commission is in Matthew 28:19–20. Paul gives it to his friend in 2 Timothy 4:2. It is as if Paul lifts up his head from his doubts.

Quote: 'To my God a heart of flame; to my fellows a heart of love; to myself a heart of steel.' (Motto of St Augustine)

Walking: a life of Christ: 'We speak in Christ' (verse 17, RSV). Speak of Jesus, the General at the front of the procession, full circle to the beginning of the reading. You could use 2 Corinthians 5:17, Philippians 1:21 or even 1 Corinthians 10:31.

Ending: Be excited, as you close, about this amazing life and the huge privilege to be walking in it. Shall we go home to be like that? Who'd like a squirt of the spray? From you – and from Jesus!

91. 'The Good, the Bad and the Ugly'

WHEN: Motivation to faith-sharing.

AIM: To bring some realism to faith-sharing by looking at the reactions Paul found to his ministry, and to see that we may encounter similar sorts of people. To encourage faith-sharing, whatever the reaction.

BIBLE READING: Acts 14:1–20.

OUTLINE:
Introduction: You could, jokingly, pose a trivia quiz question: The movies – who was Aldo Guiffré? Clue: Il Brutto. Further clue: Lee Van Cleef was Il Malo. Final clue: Clint Eastwood was Il Buono. In reverse order they were the title characters from (arguably) the best spaghetti western ever: *The Good, the Bad and the Ugly* (so Guiffré was 'the Ugly').

The point being? These are the three sorts of people we may meet if we go to share God's good news: which is what we should be doing.

Quote: 'The church exists to proclaim the Gospel.' (Archbishop Robert Runcie at NEAC, 1988)

Explain that Paul met these three sorts of people: you will show this from the reading.

The Good: Start with the positive: verse 1 shows there are good days. Comment on the word 'effectively'. You may want to draw on the good deeds which went with good words: the 'miraculous signs and wonders' (verse 3) and healings (verses 8–10).

Ask your hearers if we are like this today, or if we have tamed our words and actions. What is missing today?

Quote/Story: Thomas Aquinas, the medieval theologian, was being shown the magnificent art treasures and architecture of the Vatican by the pope, who said, 'You see, Thomas, the Church can no longer say, "Silver and gold have I none."' 'True, holy Father,' Aquinas replied, 'But neither can she say, "Rise up and walk."'

Encourage your hearers to believe in God being at work today and that 'a great number' still want to respond positively. But there are also:

The Bad: They are in verses 2 and 4. There are those who say 'No'.

Quote: 'People instinctively run away from the living God.' (Archbishop George Carey at the Evangelists' Consultation, 1992)

You could tell the weird story in verses 11–18, bringing it up to date with the odd views there are today in some New Age ideas. Think of a couple of strange notions you have heard (Easter means eggs, Hallowe'en is not about a Christian festival but pumpkins and 'trick or treat'). Again, encourage your hearers: even those who oppose us may be won round if we engage with them to sort out their misconceptions.

The Ugly: Move to verse 5 and its outcome in verse 19. There is sometimes serious opposition.

> **Quote:** 'The Christian faith is not for cowards.' (Agrippa Khathide of South Africa)

Say how privileged we are not to be physically persecuted, compared with many countries: you could use a couple of illustrations of places where it is dangerous to be a Christian. Even if we are not physically attacked, admit that there may be some verbal abuse, however gently we share our faith. Perhaps Christians are now 'politically incorrect'.

> **Quote:** 'When I give food to the poor, they call me a saint. When I ask why the poor have no food, they call me a communist.' (Don Helder Camara)

You could make reference to Ephesians 6:12.

Ending: Draw on 'as usual' in verse 1: it was the norm to faith-share. Ask if it is ours. Point out that moving on may be wise (verse 6), but we are not to quit (verse 7). Verse 20 is powerful: they go on despite the stoning. We need to go out with God's good news, however people react.

> **Quote:** 'Let us die climbing.' (Amy Carmichael)

92. Being Visible

WHEN: Faith-sharing. Short talk.

AIM: To encourage your church/Christian group both to live out and to speak out their faith.

HINT: With a short reading, this talk may not need to take long. All verses are from the reading.

BIBLE READING: Mark 4:21–25.

OUTLINE:

Introduction: You could start by saying you have a great little passage from Mark's Gospel to speak from, but the meaning is not totally clear, so you will have to give the alternatives. Joke that language is often tricky:

> **Quote/Story:** At the International Discipleship Conference in Eastbourne in 1999, a notice read: 'If you need a translation into French or Spanish, please register at the Information Desk.' Sadly, the notice was only in English. . .

Explain that there are two meanings for the verses from Mark: here are both.

Do we do what we should? Read verse 21 and say that the obvious meaning is: do we keep our Christianity hidden at home? Ask if we are Christians who are so busy with internal problems, or concerned so much with our worshipping, that we hide the light of the good news of Jesus.

> **Quote:** 'There is the reality of a world desperately needing every anointed person to preach the gospel, while the church busies itself with unending doctrinal debate over who is qualified to minister in what position. We are, in a sense, watching the house burn down while arguing about which fire truck to use.' (Sheri Benvenuti)

Say how we have been given the light of Christ, asking if we are really visible. Now to the alternative meaning:

Do we say what we should? Quote verses 21 and 22, explaining that the 'lamp' is the gospel, which Jesus brought: it is not for hiding in obscure meaning.

> **Quote/Joke:** 'Some modernistic theologians meet Jesus. "Who do you say I am?" he asks. They reply: "You are the ground of being, you are the leap of faith into the impenetrable unknown, you are the existential, un-phraseable, unverbalised, unpropositional confrontation with the infinitude of inherent, subjective experience." And Jesus says, "What?!" ' (W. A. Criswell)

Share that the message may have been obscure to the disciples when Jesus spoke, but he has now died, risen, ascended and sent his Holy Spirit: and now we have a clear message.

> **Quote:** 'The first task of the church is to call all humanity to reconciliation with God.' (Peter Coterell)

Now speak about how we will know what to say if we listen carefully in the first place.

Do we hear what we should? Use verse 24 to show that, if we listen to Jesus, the amount of attention we pay will equal what we get out, so we need to listen in. You could make something of 'consider carefully'.

> **Quote:** 'A great many people think they are thinking when they are merely rearranging their prejudices.' (William James)

Go on to verse 25: the more we give Jesus, the more he can give us. Speak of the serious warning in the second half of this verse, urging your hearers to have a real faith of their own.

Ending: Encourage your hearers to be positive in their faith, to get involved, be visible, speak clearly, listen and let Jesus speak to them, saying that they will then be good lights in a dark world.

93. Proclaiming the Gospel

WHEN: Faith-sharing.

AIM: To explain the Who? Where? What? Why? and How? of faith-sharing.

HINT: Most Christians would like to share their faith, but are not sure where to begin. This talk aims to answer their basic questions. You need to enthuse with each point, keeping things nice and simple, so there is some action as a result.

BIBLE READING: Romans 15:14–21.

OUTLINE:
Introduction: If you yourself struggle with faith-sharing (who doesn't?), admit that, when the Bible talks of sharing your faith, your reaction is often, 'Oh dear!' So today you will try to answer the basic questions we all have.

Who? Verse 15: 'You' means us all. You could draw from the all-inclusivity of Acts 1:8.

> **Quote:** 'Those who are captivated by Christ want to captivate others for Christ.' (Eric Delve)

If you are a minister or a church leader, say how the word 'me' at the end of verse 15 is you! You could draw from Revelation 1:6, saying how we are all 'priests', hence the 'duty' in verse 16. Aim to show that we are all in this together, with no exceptions.

Where do I begin? Use the lovely words in verse 15, '. . .because of the grace of God given to me'. Say how we cannot give what we have not got: Acts 3:6 is good here. Help your hearers to see that they can do it from where they are: they can share their story of knowing Jesus.

> **Quote:** 'My witness must flow not so much from my nut as from my gut – not so much from my knowledge as from my experience.' (Ian Host)

To whom? (verse 16) 'The Gentiles': that's everyone! (Except the Jews, whom Paul put as his first priority in Romans 9:11.)

> **Quote:** 'The Kingdom is open to everyone, irrespective of their position in the kingdoms of the world.' (Archbishop George Carey, from 'Jesus 2000, The Archbishop of Canterbury's Millennium Message')

It would be good to draw on the lovely words of verse 21, quoting Isaiah 52:15, the context of which is Jesus dying on the cross. Urge your hearers to share this most of all. You could refer to John 10:16, again with the context of John 10:11.

What? Enthuse about the simplicity of verse 16, 'Proclaiming the gospel of God'.

Quote: 'He who will restore to men the primitive principles of Christianity will alter the face of the world.' (Benjamin Franklin, former president of the USA)

Speak of the danger of our for ever getting sidetracked by peripheral matters instead of getting to the heart of the Christian message: God's love, Christ's death (for our forgiveness) and resurrection, the Holy Spirit bringing new life, heaven.

Encourage the accentuation of the positive.

Quote: 'This is the first time in nine years I have been asked to give a word of encouragement.' (Ven. Hugh Buckingham, Archdeacon of Beverley, at a church mission commissioning service)

Why? Still in verse 16, take the second half of the verse. Isn't it lovely? You could draw from Ephesians 4:12, about building up Christ's body. Ask your hearers who they would like to offer to God.

Quote: 'I believe people haven't rejected Jesus. They haven't heard of him in their language, in their culture, in a way that they can respond to.' (Alan Smith, former Rector of Rushden)

How? Be sure to emphasise that it is through the Holy Spirit's power, not by our skills: 'Sanctified by the Holy Spirit' (verse 16). You could bring in Philippians 4:13.

Ending: Tell your hearers to go for it and to be sure to give God the glory (verse 17), using Psalm 115:1 if you want a back-up.

FAITH-SHARING – TO THEM

94. The Greatest Offer in the World

WHEN: Pubs. Prisons. Youth event.

AIM: To share the greatness of the offer from Jesus of new life, including the challenges which go with this.

HINT: This is a very straightforward talk, based on one verse. If you could learn it and its context, you could give it almost anywhere without the need for notes. Or you could simply read the verse from a small New Testament and speak extemporarily. Always remember, most 'extemporary' talks are the ones we prepare most carefully!

KEY VERSE: Mark 1:15.

BIBLE READING: Mark 1:14–20 (for context). If you need a second reading, you could use Jeremiah 18:1–8 (for the section on 'I will make you').

OUTLINE:
Introduction: Talk about good offers which have catches when you examine them. Today you have the greatest offer in the world – and there are one or two catches in this one, too.

What's the offer? Here's another question: if you'd been Jesus, and you'd waited 30 years to preach, what would your first sermon have been? Here it is: quote Mark 1:14–15 and show the follow-up in verses 16 and 17. What's he saying?

1. **Repent.** An amazing opportunity to face up to the wrong in our lives and deliberately turn from it to be forgiven. So much better than just being sorry: 'repent' means to turn away from sin by an act of will.

   Quote: 'Repentance – the Bible commands it, our wickedness demands it, justice requires it, Christ preached it, God expects it.' (Billy Graham)

2. **Believe the good news.** The news is sensational. Jesus has paid for our sins, so we can repent. He has bought our forgiveness on the cross and brought new life back from the grave. By his Holy Spirit we can be made new.

3. **I will make you.** Jeremiah 18:1–4 works well in conjunction with Mark 1:17. This includes reaching out to others – a challenge as well as a privilege. You could draw from 2 Timothy 2:21.

Who gives the offer? Verse 14 – 'Jesus', 'the Son of God' (verse 1).

Quotes: 'What we want you to know is Jesus. When you know him, you know all.' (J. Denham-Smith, *The Gospel in Hosea*)

'We can never hear too much of Christ.' (J. C. Ryle, *Knots Untied*)

It is a personal call from the greatest person who ever lived on planet earth. Revelation 3:20 would not be out of place here. Speak of how ultimately special Jesus is.

When is the offer? It is now: verse 15, with 2 Corinthians 6:2. The word 'near' is translated 'at hand' in the RSV.

We may or may not be living in days at the end of the earth's history, but either way each one of us will have ended our lives here on earth sooner or later: we must respond to the offer while we have time.

Quotes: 'We are entering the Messianic era.' (Rabbi Shelomo Goren, one-time chief rabbi to the Israeli forces)

'The prophetic clock of God is ticking while history moves inexorably toward the final climax.' (Dr Carl Henry, one-time editor of *Christianity Today*)

For whom is the offer? John 7:37 is a great answer. The message of Mark 1 was, and is, for everyone. It is for your hearers right now.

Ending: Say how honoured you are to have accepted the offer of forgiveness and new life from Jesus. Ask who will receive the offer today. Give people the opportunity to say 'Yes'.

95. Three-way Christianity

WHEN: Meals. Pubs.

AIM: To explain what Christianity really is. To give a positive talk on what it means to live the Christian life.

HINT: Make this an enthusiastic talk, showing how great it is to know Jesus, because he changes our approach in our relationships. So often Christians are seen as having a negative approach to life: try to give the opposite angle with this talk.

KEY VERSE: Romans 14:17: 'For the kingdom of God is not a matter of eating and drinking, but of righteousness, peace and joy in the Holy Spirit.'

BIBLE READING: Romans 14:13–18 (or to verse 23).

OUTLINE:

Introduction: What Christianity is *not*. Explain how, when Paul wrote, people got uptight about what they should eat and drink, especially regarding meat offered to the false Roman gods and then sold at the market. He's not saying 'don't bother' (compare 1 Corinthians 10:31) and he's not encouraging drinking too much (Ephesians 5:18).

Don't dwell too long on history! Joke how Christians are often seen as those who love to say 'No'! Christianity is seen as a set of rules: 'Do this, don't do that.' Give a couple of examples from your own upbringing.

So what *is* Christianity? It is all about relationships – the three big ones in our lives:

With God: righteousness: The impossible (see Romans 3:10) becomes possible through Jesus.

> **Quote/Story:** St Jerome wished, one Christmas night, to give a present to the infant Christ. First he offered his translations of the Scriptures: the gift was not accepted. He next offered his efforts for the conversion of his friends: also refused. He offered the virtues he possessed: another no. 'Jerome,' said the Lord, 'it is your sins I wish for. Give them to me that I may pardon them.'

Use the argument set out in Romans 3:22–24 to show how Jesus has died to obtain for us a right relationship with God. Of course, this will affect the things we do (and don't do): Romans 12:1. But these will be done from love, not coercion.

With others: peace: Christians enter a new family (see Romans 12:5).

> **Quote:** 'An unconquerable fellowship.' (J. B. Phillips)

This leads to us being kind and positive. Verses 13 and 15 could be referred to, with some of your examples of us caring for our Christian brothers and sisters.

Say, with a smile, that this is not always easy – some of us are difficult to live with!

Quote/Story: Antoine de Saint-Exupéry, in his delightful children's book *The Little Prince*, has a flower who talks with the prince. The prince asks her about the crawly things on her, to which the flower replies, 'I must endure the presence of two or three caterpillars if I wish to become acquainted with the butterflies.'

With ourselves: joy:

Quotes: 'Despair is such a waste of time when there is joy, and lack of faith is such a waste of time when there is God.' (Larry Burner)

'If they were to put me into a barrel, I would shout "glory" through the bunghole! Praise the Lord!' (Billy Bray, Cornish preacher)

This is 'joy in the Holy Spirit': Jesus, by his Spirit, enables us to look at ourselves in the mirror and know we're OK. Romans 15:13 is good here.

Ending: Verse 18 is the end of the sentence from our key verse: isn't that what we all want? Lead your hearers in a prayer to enter into this new relationship with God, others and themselves.

96. Which Side?

WHEN: Sports event.

WHO: Non-Christians. Men. Young people.

AIM: To encourage people to come over to the side of Jesus Christ.

HINT: This talk is based on the dramatic and ultimately rather bloodthirsty incident in the reading. The key is that there was a choice then and there is now: there is no need to dwell on the slaughter. You will need to be aware of the background, which is in Exodus 19, the following chapters being the giving of the laws.

BIBLE READING: Exodus 32:1–29 (long, but all needed).

OUTLINE:
Way in: It would help if you support a football team, or are proud of where you were born. You could then begin by asking, 'Who supports [name your team]?' or 'Who comes from [name your county/area or origin]?' Raised hands will bring cheers and jeers! Now explain that you could do the same by asking who belongs to Jesus Christ: say you won't now, but that's where you are heading. You'd like to tell a true story:

The choice long ago: Tell the story as graphically as you can: Moses leading well over two million from Egypt (Exodus 12:37 – 600,000 men, plus women and children), the sea parting, the journey – and the need for laws. Come to chapter 19, with Moses telling the people to 'be good' while he was away. Now come to the reading, with the people stopping believing in God as he really is: going for a calf of gold.

> **Quote:** 'People think that when they don't believe in God they believe nothing, but the fact is they'll believe in anything.' (G. K. Chesterton)

Dramatically describe the making of the golden calf, leading to wild and immoral behaviour, with chaos in the camp.

> **Quote:** 'So, once again, you chose for yourself – and opened the door to chaos. The chaos you always become whenever God's hand does not rest upon your head.' (Dag Hammarskjøld, former Secretary General of the United Nations)

Come to the great call of Moses in verse 26, with its limited response: God's call to be on his side. You may, or may not, wish to mention the punishment for those who stayed (verse 27): the point is the choice and the decision.

The choice today: Point out that Moses isn't here – but Jesus is. He is so much greater (compare Matthew 12:41–42). He calls us.

> **Quote:** 'In our country today there's too much sitting on the fence and funking a decision about religion. I hear people say to me, almost as if they're proud of it, "I'm not

a religious man," almost as if they're saying, "I'm proud to say I've got pneumonia." Very often this means a lazy agnosticism which hasn't been thought through at all. Christianity hasn't been tried and found wanting – too often it hasn't been tried at all. I don't believe there is any need to compare with this – an open, proud allegiance to Christ, his standards, his way of life, his values in the company of his church. This, I believe, is the great need of our nation today.' (Donald Coggan, when Archbishop of York, addressing the Law Society Conference, October 1969)

Speak of Jesus keeping God's law, paying on the cross for our breaking it, calling to us, 'Come to me' (Matthew 11:28). It is a matter of life or death.

Quotes: 'Hell or heaven, and heaven requires a reservation.' (Dr E. V. Hill)

'The issue is now clear. It is between light and darkness, and everyone must choose his side.' (G. K. Chesterton, on his deathbed)

Go back to the reading, to show the open step from the tents (verse 26). The Saviour calls us out to forgive us, give us new life, change us into God's people.

Quote: 'The heart of Christ's message is extremely simple: an encounter with God, a real one, means change.' (David Wilkerson, *The Cross and the Switchblade*)

Ending: Make your call, with the lovely promise in John 6:37. Moses dared – will you dare to call people to belong to Jesus?

97. Right Turn

WHEN: Short talk. Pubs. Open-air. Youth event.

AIM: To show how we need to turn round and go God's way.

HINT: How much of what follows is included in your talk depends on both the length of the talk and the audience. If this is in the open air, pick out the key points and keep it short. Only if you are with church people will you need to quote verses: otherwise they are your guide only.

BIBLE READING: Ezekiel 18:25–33 (the key verses are 30–32).

OUTLINE:

Introduction: Everyone has a friend or relative (or it might even be you) who has no sense of direction. Relate a humorous/horror story of misguided navigation, resulting in the need for a complete turnaround to get to the desired journey's end. ('When I said "turn left" ten miles ago, I meant "right". Please explain that to the police officer.')

Going away: We all take the wrong road in life. Using verses 30–32, you could explain (briefly) how God's people got lost from God long ago because of their 'offences'. Give some examples of how we do this in our lives and in our world today.

Quote: 'Western civilisation suffers from a strong sense of moral and spiritual exhaustion. Having constructed a society of unprecedented sophistication, convenience and prosperity, nobody can remember what it was supposed to be for.' (Clifford Longley)

We have gone the wrong way and got lost. Now we can't see the right way because of our sin, hurts, pain and bereavements.

Quote: 'It is nearly evening and the day is almost over. Stay with me, Lord, for night has fallen and, too often, it is dark in my heart.' (Michel Quoist, *Meet Christ and Live*)

We have been conned by our postmodernistic society into believing that everything is relative: but there are absolutes. God is real. We are going the wrong way. We are heading for disaster. We need an answer.

Quote: 'There is a better way to live our life,
And I must find it if I can.'
(The Flying Pickets, song 'So Close')

Coming back: You could quote verses 30–32 again – the answer is there: 'Repent . . . turn away . . . get a new heart and a new spirit . . . Repent and live!'

We have to turn from our way to the way of Jesus: John 14:6. You could explain how, after Jesus had spoken those words, he went out to die on the cross. We can 'cross' to the right road at that cross.

Speak of Jesus' great sacrifice and of his rising again to make the new road open.

Verse 31 shows the problem: our pride stops us from turning.

> **Quote:** 'The proud human heart is revealed. We insist on paying for what we have done. We cannot stand the humiliation of acknowledging our bankruptcy and allow somebody else to pay for us. The notion that this somebody else should be God himself is just too much to take. We would rather perish than repent, rather lose ourselves than humble ourselves.' (John Stott, *The Cross of Christ*)

Yet, if we do 'repent', then we 'live' (verse 32). We have made the right turn. We get 'a new heart and a new spirit' (verse 31). We are heading for heaven!

Ending: It's time to make this right turn. Invite your hearers to do just that and give them space to do so.

98. Quo Vadis?

WHEN: 'Tricky Questions' session. Advent. Sports event.

WHO: Seekers.

AIM: This is a 'bite the bullet' talk when we dare to face our ultimate destiny: where are we going? 'Quo Vadis?' – 'Where are you going?' We'd all like to know!

EXPLANATION: This talk is not based on a specific Bible reading, although Ephesians 2:1–10 would work. Instead, it draws on several scriptures to answer some basic questions.

CHALLENGE: The question is, who dares preach this sort of talk in days when its content is less than popular among Christians?

OUTLINE:
Introduction: John Bunyan, author of *A Pilgrim's Progress*, and Winston Churchill both challenge us:

Quotes: 'Will you leave your sins and go to heaven, or keep your sins and go to hell?' These were the words which changed Bunyan's life when he heard them on a village green at the age of 16.

'The moral landslide in Great Britain can be traced to the fact that heaven and hell are no longer proclaimed throughout the land.' (Winston Churchill)

Where can you go? Check the answers from Moses in Deuteronomy 30:19, Jeremiah (Jeremiah 21:8) and Jesus in Matthew 7:13–14. The last one is key: there are only two destinies and only one leads to God, as Jesus said in John 14:6.

A narrow choice? Life often presents such 'narrowness': you could use examples from driving (just too close and then the crash); sport (was the ball over the line?); interviews (nearly got the job).

While never threatening, don't ever pretend that the negative does not exist: check Proverbs 14:12.

Quote: 'Take seriously the Biblical description of those without Christ.' (Julian Charley)

Where do you want to go?

Quote: ' "Can you tell me the way?" asked Alice. "That all depends on where you want to go," replied the Cheshire cat.' (Lewis Carroll, *Alice in Wonderland*)

Show how the 'way of the world' is often the easy option, pleasing oneself. God's way is frequently harder and more challenging (Matthew 7:14; Mark 8:34).

Where are you now? On one road or the other.

Quote: 'There be two manner of men. Some there be that be not justified, nor regenerated, nor yet in a state of salvation; that is to say, not God's servants. They lack the renovation or regeneration; they be not yet come to Christ.' (A delightfully old-style way of expressing it by Bishop Hugh Latimer, 1552)

Unless we have been specifically rescued, we are going away from God.
Every day we continue our journeys.

Quotes/Story: Philip of Macedonia (father of Alexander the Great) commanded one slave to stand before him every day and say, 'Philip, remember you must die.'

'Death – wherever we're going. Maybe I'll see you there, 'cos I'm not ready yet.' (Donovan, speaking 'In Concert', BBC2, 1972)

How can you cross over? At the cross. Jesus has come looking for us (Luke 19:10). He calls us over (Matthew 11:28). The Ephesians reading would work well here. We can get a transfer. Colossians 1:12–13 in the RSV uses the words 'transferred us': an excellent quote.

Where do you go from today? Accentuate the positive, using Ephesians 6:10, Hebrews 13:5 and Matthew 28:20.

Ending: This a 'come on over' call. Make it!

99. Eternal Life

WHEN: General use.

WHO: Non-Christians. Church members. New Christians.

AIM: To show the vital choice we have to make in trusting our lives to Jesus Christ and the eternal consequences of this.

HINT: The story of the rich man and Lazarus is one of the most famous Jesus told. By itself it can be somewhat threatening. This talk therefore tries to give a balance by linking it with a delightful letter of Paul's, to enable the positive to be emphasised.

BIBLE READINGS: 2 Timothy 1:1–14; Luke 16:19–31.

OUTLINE:
Introduction: You could get into this talk by saying that there are some things we talk about which matter a little, others matter a lot, but one or two things may matter for ever – and you have one of those today. It would get attention! You want to say two things:

God's life is a gift: Point to the fact that there is an eternal life, not as a threat but as a joyful reality. What is the sense in living only for the here and now? We are greater than that. Now share the good news that this is a precious gift from God, using the Timothy reading at verses 9 and 10. Speak of how wonderful these words are, and how Jesus has bought this gift by his death on the cross.

> **Quote:** 'Upon a life I did not live, upon a death I did not die, I hang my whole eternity.' (John Calvin)

Ask if your hearers know how you get this life. You could share how Timothy found out – from his relatives (verse 5), posing the question as to where the men were. . . You could then ask whom your hearers have heard from – grandma, a friend, a book; going on to say that, whoever we hear from, we need to trust Jesus (verse 13b) and know the Holy Spirit (verse 14). When we do, we are able. . .

> **Quote:** 'To live life properly, and meet death securely.' (Dave Burton)

It matters for ever: Now we go to the Luke story. Be a little melodramatic, indicating that you have the most serious story Jesus ever told – and tell it, briefly but well. Now ask: what is Jesus telling us? Here are a few pointers for you to draw from:

1. Share the big twenty-first-century danger of living for today only and not thinking in a 'for-ever' way: is it because we are afraid?

   > **Quote:** 'Old age isn't so bad when you consider the alternative.' (Maurice Chevalier)

2. The good news for you to give is that there is a place of love, comfort and beauty.

Quote/Story: Dietrich Bonhoeffer was hanged by the Nazis on Easter Day, 1945. He wrote in his diary that morning, 'Death is the supreme festival on the road to freedom.'

3. Tell your hearers the whole truth – there is a place of terrible separation from God. If this is only a picture, what is it depicting? Say how you certainly don't like the sound of it, and don't want to go there.

   Quote: 'How do people face death without God? Why do they punish themselves?' (Mike Dewsbery, as he was dying of cancer)

4. If we live for self, we will not go to God. Ask your hearers if they are building on themselves, or on Jesus.

   Quote: 'You, have you built well, have you forgotten the cornerstone? Talking of right relations of men, but not of relations of men to God.' (T. S. Eliot, from 'The Rock', Chorus II)

5. Be sure to say how God gives us every chance (verse 31): Jesus is alive, to give us new life.

6. Whatever anyone says, this story shows there is no second chance after death. Is that why we are scared?

   Quote: 'I'm scared of no one. I'm only scared of death.' (Muhammad Ali, boxer)

Ending: Urge your hearers to have the faith of Timothy, not the stupidity of the rich man.

   Quote/Story: Michael Cassidy tells of the son who telegrammed his mother, 'Failed every exam. Prepare Dad.' Mother replied, 'Dad prepared. Prepare yourself.'

100. Lady in Red

WHEN: General use. Ladies' meetings.

AIM: To show how our sins may be forgiven and we can know new life in Jesus.

HINT: The talk, despite the title sounding like a song by Chris de Burgh, is partially based on Rahab, who lived in Jericho until its walls fell down. It would be wise to be acquainted with the whole incident. The passage does not have to be read out unless in a church service which requires one.

BIBLE READING: Joshua 2:1–21.

OUTLINE:

Introduction: You could open by talking, either seriously or jocularly, about 'political correctness'; for example, not allowing coffee to be offered 'black or white' these days, but 'without or with milk'. We speakers have to be careful what we say! Then go on to say that we talk of evil and good as being 'black or white' and there's a danger of insulting people with this. Then say we are wrong with both words: the Bible talks of evil using another colour.

Sin is red: Quote from parts of Isaiah 1:18: 'Your sins are like scarlet . . . they are red as crimson.' You could say how it has been unpopular to talk of 'wrong and right'. But these days, we need to.

> **Quote:** 'Concepts such as good and evil have gone out of fashion, but we must relearn these terms.' (*The Jerusalem Post*, 11 September 2001, after the 9/11 events in New York)

Have you got an example of some red fruit staining a table cloth? Or of a food (like beetroot) causing an indelible stain? A red example would be the best.

> **Quote:** 'Scarlet and crimson were the only two "fast" dyes in the ancient world.' (Swithin Manoharan, referring to the Isaiah 1 verse)

The problem is, how can we remove the red stain of sin in our lives?

> **Quote:** 'The significant problems we face cannot be solved by the thinking which created them.' (Albert Einstein)

The answer is red: If you are a blood donor (or know one) this quote is excellent:

> **Quote:** 'Remember, by donating blood, you can actually help someone to live. It's the most important gift you can give.' (Belinda Phipps, South Thames Transfusion Service)

Now you can quote the whole of Isaiah 1:18. Also, 1 John 1:7 is terrific, especially the way it speaks of 'cleansing'.

Quote: 'Out of love our Lord took us to himself; because he loved us and it was God's will, our Lord Jesus Christ gave his life blood for us – he gave his body for our body, his soul for our soul.' (Bishop Clement of Rome, died c.AD 95)

Now you can tell the story of Rahab, the 'scarlet woman' (as prostitutes are called), one of the enemy in Jericho, and how she protected the spies of God's people and hung the 'scarlet cord' (Joshua 2:21) in the window. Joshua 6:22–23 shows her being rescued when the city fell.

Her restoration from 'scarlet woman' was total: she is a 'woman of faith' in that great 'people of faith' chapter (check Hebrews 11:31) and is in the lineage of Jesus (Matthew 1:5). Show how she was saved by the red cord and how Jesus saves us by his red blood. We get new life for old.

Quote: 'The life he gives if we keep his company.' (Oliver Howarth)

Ending: 'Put on your red dress' is a line from a song. If you are not speaking exclusively to ladies, adapt the expression! You could refer back to Isaiah 1:18 or 1 John 1:7 to invite your hearers to have their stains washed away.

Situations Index

[Numbers refer to talk numbers not pages]

Scripture Index